"This devotional speaks directly ...
Papa. I love how it brings about a purposeful focus in strategic prayer to end abortion."
~Jennifer Milbourn, Vacuum Aspiration Abortion Survivor, Abortion Survivors Network

"Cheryl's book helps people with the most powerful weapons to help end abortion: prayer, God's truth, and worship! She leads people through their quiet time with the Lord; helps them prepare their hearts to go to battle for the unborn, mothers and fathers; and shows how to worship Jesus during the battle. I love her kindness and heart behind this book. What a great guide to help our hearts stay on track to be bold in our prayers to end abortion but also love others well."
~Serena Dyksen, Founder and Author of *She Found His Grace* SerenaDyksen.com

"A fresh approach to changing abortion law forever. Cheryl Krichbaum introduces worship as the battle plan to stop the practice that destroys millions of lives every year: lives of babies, mothers, fathers, and practitioners."
~Faye Bryant, Speaker, Life Purpose Coach, and Author of *Coffee, Bible, Journal;* The Grandma, Mom, and Me Saga; and *Ramblings from the Shower* FayeBryant.com

"Written from the heart of a woman who has experienced the healing power of our grace-filled, love-motivated, powerful Heavenly Father, *Worship to End Abortion* beckons the reader with the life-changing, life-healing power of Jesus Christ. This scripture-rich guide is anointed with hope. Cheryl is your seasoned tour guide on a journey of engaging the Lord in worship to bring about the end of what nearly was the end of her. More Christians need to be equipped for spiritual battle, and Cheryl's devotional guide will help many confidently put on their armor!"
~Briana Nei, Founder of Revealed Ministries for Women, Speaker, and Author of *Revealed in Ephesians: The Mystery of Who I Am in Christ* BrianaNei.com

WORSHIP
TO END ABORTION
Your Prayer Guide

CHERYL KRICHBAUM

AUTHOR
ACADEMY elite

Printed in the United States of America

Published by Author Academy Elite
P.O. Box 43, Powell, OH 43035
AuthorAcademyElite.com

Library of Congress Control Number: 2020916798

Paperback ISBN: 978-1-64746-486-8
Hardcover ISBN: 978-1-64746-487-5
E-book ISBN: 978-1-64746-488-2

Scripture quotations marked (NASB) are taken from the New American Standard Bible® Copyright© 1960, 1962, 1963, 1968, 1971, 1972, 1973, 1975, 1977, 1995 by The Lockman Foundation. Used by permission.

Scripture quotations marked (ESV) are from The ESV® Bible (The Holy Bible, English Standard Version®), copyright © 2001 by Crossway, a publishing ministry of Good News Publishers. Used by permission. All rights reserved.

Scripture quotations marked (NKJV) are taken from the New King James Version®. Copyright © 1982 by Thomas Nelson. Used by permission. All rights reserved.

Scripture quotations marked (NLT) are taken from the Holy Bible, New Living Translation, copyright ©1996, 2004, 2015 by Tyndale House Foundation. Used by permission of Tyndale House Publishers, a Division of Tyndale House Ministries, Carol Stream, Illinois 60188. All rights reserved.

Scripture quotations marked (AMP) are taken from the Amplified® Bible (AMP), Copyright © 2015 by The Lockman Foundation. Used by permission. www.Lockman.org.

for

Joy Marie

d. June 18, 1987

&

Andrew Towler

who re-introduced me to the power of worship

Contents

Introduction

Boot Camp

Interlude

History Lessons

Battle

Appendices

Prayer List

Boot Camp

Interlude

History Lessons

Battle

Becoming Worship Warriors in the Spiritual Battle of Abortion

Abortion is a spiritual battle.

Because abortion[a] evokes strong feelings about politics, women's rights, and defenseless pre-born babies, we often forget about the spiritual battle. We choose to get angry and neglect to put on our Armor of God and battle in prayer.

Changing abortion laws will not end abortion. Yes, fewer women would abort if it were illegal. As a post-abortive woman myself, I can unequivocally say that I would have given birth if abortion had been illegal in 1987. In contrast, Abby Johnson has said that she would have had illegal abortions. Without a change in our hearts, abortion will continue to be a "solution" women and men pursue.

---

a   Throughout this book, the term *abortion* means *elective abortion* because, unfortunately, our dictionaries define *miscarriage* as *spontaneous abortion*. If I were the editor of the dictionary, I would define *miscarriage* as *the death of a pre-born baby without the assistance of people* and *abortion* as *the murder of a pre-born baby.*

If abortion were to become illegal today, it would go underground. Not only would we have abortions in facilities similar to Kermit Gosnell's[a] but also a new illegal drug trade. People feel so strongly about abortion that changing the laws could be a precursor for a second civil war. Changing the laws would be a small win compared to making abortion unthinkable.

To make abortion unthinkable, we Christians need to educate ourselves, teach others, and be worship warriors in this spiritual battle.

Ending abortion starts with us. The more love, joy, and peace Christians share with women and men, the less they will choose abortion and the extramarital sex that creates the "need" for abortion.

> *The fruit of the* [Holy] Spirit *is* love, joy, peace, *patience, kindness, goodness, faithfulness, gentleness, self-control; against such things there is no law.* (Galatians 5:22-23 NASB, emphasis mine)

We do not end abortion through politics but by the power of God at work within us.

> *Now to Him who is able to [carry out His purpose and] do superabundantly more than all that we dare ask or think [infinitely beyond our greatest prayers, hopes, or dreams],* according to His power that is at work within us, *to Him be the glory in the church and in Christ Jesus throughout all generations forever and ever. Amen.* (Ephesians 3:20-21 AMP, emphasis mine)

In this book, you will learn:

- How to use God's armor to protect yourself in battle
- Why worship is a powerful weapon

---

a GosnellMovie.com
Ann McElhinney and Phelim McAleer, *Gosnell: The Untold Story of America's Most Prolific Serial Killer* (Washington, DC: Regnery Publishing, 2018).

- Why women see abortion as a justice issue for themselves
- What is the history of abortion in the U.S.
- What happens to women and men spiritually when they choose abortion
- How to make a difference through worshipful prayer, giving, and speaking the truth in love

Each section includes a Bible story, its application to the abortion conversation, and suggested prayers.

Pray the 40 daily prayers word-for-word or use them as a guide for your own prayers using the provided scriptural references.

Start your prayers the way you want.[a] End your prayers the way you want.[b] I don't care what denomination you follow or don't follow. I simply ask for Christ's disciples to stand firm[c] as one in Him.[d]

You may pray these prayers anytime, of course, but I hope that you will also pray in concert with the fall and spring **40 Days for Life** campaigns.

40 Days for Life is an internationally coordinated 40-day campaign that aims to end abortion locally through prayer and fasting, community outreach, and a peaceful all-day vigil in front of abortion businesses.[e]

The fall campaign begins on the 4th Wednesday in September. The spring campaign begins on Ash Wednesday.[f] Join me and

---

a   The name of the Lord is a strong tower; The righteous runs into it and is safe. (Proverbs 18:10 NASB)

b   "If you ask the Father for anything in My name, He will give it to you." (John 16:23b NASB)

c   Ephesians 6:10, 13, 14

d   John 17:11

e   40 Days for Life (website), "About Overview: Helping to End the Injustice of Abortion." Accessed July 1, 2020. https://www.40daysforlife.com/about-overview.aspx.

f   on the Roman calendar, not the Orthodox calendar

others like yourself on social media for group prayer, additional teachings, and worship parties.

@CherylKrichbaum on Facebook, Instagram, and Twitter

@MybodyMyworship on YouTube

Make this prayer guide your daily devotional or read it with your small group. Invite your friends!

Let us be worship warriors against this present darkness and agape[a] love warriors for the people on the earth. Let us pray for life on earth as it is in heaven.[b]

I want to do one last edit of this book before sending it to print. I should get a review copy to make sure that it's perfect. *But there's no time!* I sense an urgency to pray and worship right now in the 40 days leading up to the 2020 elections even though this book does not promote political parties or candidates.

If you find mistakes, please send them to me through my website at MybodyMyworship.com, and I will credit you on the acknowlegments page of the next printing.

In Christ,

Cheryl

---

a   Greek, the original language of the New Testament, has multiple words that we translate into English as the word *love*. *Philo, eros,* and *agape* are three well-known Greek words for *love:*
  - *Philo* translates to *brotherly love.* You'll find it in *Philadelphia,* the City of Brotherly Love. *Philo* is also one of the words for *love* in John 21:15-17 (The first two times, Jesus asks Peter, "Do you *agape* me?" and Peter responds, "Yes, Lord, You know that I *philo* You.")
  - *Eros* is from the Greek god Eros, which the Romans called Cupid. It translates to *lust* or *desire.* You'll find it in the words *erotic* and *erotica.* Today when we talk about *making love,* we mean *eros.* The word *eros* is not in the Bible.
  - In contrast, *agape* means *fond of, to love dearly;* it is a *deliberate, mindful love.* When the Apostle John says, "God is *agape*" (1 John 4:8, 16), he's saying that God is deliberately and mindfully loving us dearly.
  If we're to be like God and make Him known to the world, then we need to love like Him.
b   Matthew 6:10

Boot Camp

DAY 1

Put on Your Armor of God

J esus, the One from above,[a] open my mind to understand the Scriptures.[b]

Suit Up
Ephesians 6:10-20

"I am not afraid… I was born to do this."
~Joan of Arc

As she covered her feet with leather and fastened plate armor over her legs, perhaps Joan of Arc said, "I will stand firm in the Lord's ways and trust in Him always. With His peace in my heart, I stand ready. May the whole infantry stand ready for peace."

As her breastplate and backplate were set in place, perhaps she said, "Forgive my sins, my Lord. Give me a clean heart and renew a steadfast spirit within me.[c] With this breastplate, I guard

---

a   John 8:38
b   Luke 24:45
c   Psalm 51:10

3

my heart for everything I do flows from it.[a] Lord, thank You for protecting all my vital organs, especially my lungs through which I inhale Your Breath[b] of life."

Perhaps she said, "May the belt of truth, my Lord, hold everything together" as the waistband was fastened.

As she took up her helmet, perhaps she said, "The knowledge of Christ's sacrifice so that I may have eternal life protects my every thought from fear of evil for You are Lord of heaven and earth."

As she took up her shield, perhaps she said, "With this shield, I deflect every fiery dart for the enemy cannot distract me from my mission."

As she took up her short sword, perhaps she said, "Work through me, Lord, to defeat every enemy that dares to get close enough. I am on a mission, and I will not be deterred."

The Real Enemy

We may not be putting on actual armor as Joan of Arc did, but we certainly need to prepare ourselves for battle.

However, we must remember that elected officials, abortion facility staff, celebrity post-abortive women, and rich men and women who fund political campaigns are not the real enemy, for our struggle is not against flesh and blood but against the spiritual forces of darkness.[c] Even though we see these people as

---

a   Proverbs 4:23
b   In both the Old Testament Hebrew and the New Testament Greek, the word *Spirit* means *breath*, so *Holy Spirit* is *Holy Breath*.
c   Ephesians 6:12

the faces of the pro-abortion movement, let us not forget they are hired soldiers who believe the devil's lies.

> *Jesus said, "The devil… was a murderer from the beginning and does not stand in the truth because there is no truth in him. Whenever he speaks a lie, he speaks from his own nature, for he is a liar and the father of lies." (John 8:44 NASB)*

The devil does not want people to do God's will or to fulfill their purposes.

We do not win this war by attacking people. When we attack people, we are not doing God's will because we are called to love our neighbors.[a] We must fight against the devil with the best weapon there is—God. God is love.[b] God is truth.[c] God is life,[d] and all people throughout the world are offered the gift of eternal life through Christ:

> *"The gift of God is eternal life in Christ Jesus our Lord." (John 6:23)*

No matter how angry people make us, we must respond to them with love and also respond to the thief who comes to kill, steal, and destroy[e] with the sword of the Spirit.[f]

This is the mission if you choose to accept it: *love people* while *battling evil.*

> *This is the mission if you choose to accept it: love people while battling evil.*

Do not join this battle without your armor. The devil will attack you, so do not enter battle unprotected. Be like Joan of Arc and suit up with the *Day* 1 prayer (on page 6) or another Armor of God prayer.

---

a   Matthew 22:39 (part two of the Greatest Commandment)
b   1 John 4:8, 16
c   John 14:6
d   John 14:6
e   John 10:10
f   Ephesians 6:17

Suggested Prayers

Day 1

Ephesians 6:10-18, Proverbs 18:10

Lord, I praise you that I am strong in You and that I am in the power of Your might. Today, I put on the whole armor that You gave me so that I am able to stand against the schemes, strategies, and deceits of the devil. I take up the whole armor so that I am able to withstand evil, having done all that crisis demands, to stand victorious.

Thank You for girding my waist with truth. I confess my sins to You now so that my breastplate of righteousness is securely in place, protecting all my vital organs. Thank You that my feet are firmly grounded with the gospel of peace.

Thank You for reminding me throughout the day to defend myself by using the shield of faith to quench all the fiery darts of the wicked one. Thank You for my helmet of salvation, which protects my mind. Thank You for the sword of the Spirit, the word of God, my only offensive piece of armor.

Thank You for reminding me to pray and ask in the Spirit throughout the day, staying alert for all of Your people.

Prayer for 40 Days for Life

Lord, I stand firm for those who are praying and counseling at abortion facilities around the world. Remind them to put on their armor every day so that they withstand and stand victorious.

I praise You for girding these prayer warriors with the truth. Protect their hearts and minds. Thank you for grounding them in the gospel of peace.

Give each of them strong shields to quench every fiery dart of wickedness. Thank you for equipping them with the sword of the Spirit.

Your name is a strong tower, Lord. The righteous run inside it and are safe. We bring you the 40 Days for Life prayer warriors. Thank You for keeping them safe. Standing firm in Your name we pray, Amen.

Sleeping Well

Not only suit up in the morning, but prepare yourself to sleep well. Once I learned to suit up in the morning, I began to experience spiritual attacks in the night. I would wake up several times per night or would wake up from a bad dream. Nights are vulnerable times for me. Let me share with you my strategies for sleeping well.

First, before bed, I pray the Day 1 prayer.

Second, I pray that God would show me every door and window of my "spiritual house" that is not locked down tightly to keep evil out. I have had dreams in which I am scurrying around my house locking all the doors and windows to prevent evil from entering. The dream is recurring. Sometimes, evil managed to get into a door that I neglected to lock. One time, I dreamt that I invited someone into my house, but my guard dog wouldn't let him in.

Now, in addition to praying that I am protected by my spiritual armor, I also thank God for showing me every door and window that I need to lock so that evil cannot enter.

Third, I listen to Christian praise or meditative music as I fall asleep.

Fourth, if I wake up with a bad dream, I do some self-examination to see if I have unconfessed sin. If I had an angry dream, then I likely have pent-up anger for someone I need to forgive. That's when I tell God that I'm sorry for letting anger become bitterness, and I forgive the person at whom I'm mad.

With nightly practice, I now sleep well. I pray that these strategies help you suit up for good sleep!

DAYS 2-3

Believe

J esus, our Hope,[a] open my mind to understand the Scriptures.[b]

Desperate
Mark 9:14-29

"Husband, this man from Nazareth heals people! A paralyzed man walks.[c] A withered hand stretched and restored.[d] I heard he even cast out a legion of demons from a man among the Gerasenes.[e] Maybe… maybe he can heal our son!"

"Where is he?" the husband asked desperately. The man picked up his son and ran. His wife hurriedly followed.

"Those men! Those men follow the man Jesus," the mother called to her husband.

"Where is your leader?" the father asked nine disciples. "The healer. Where is He? He must heal our son!"

"He is not here."

---

a   1 Timothy 1:1
b   Luke 24:45
c   Mark 2:2-5, 11-12
d   Mark 3:3, 5
e   Mark 5:1-13

"Then you cast out the demons from my son! You are His disciples. Certainly, He taught you to do this!"

Some scribes overheard and stepped in, saying, "The One they call Jesus, He does not heal."

"He does," said Andrew.

"We've seen Him heal many," Matthew said.

"He even raised Jairus' daughter,"[a] Philip said.

Simon the Zealot said, "Let us cast out this demon as the Teacher taught us."

Each of the nine disciples tried to cast out the demon but could not.

"Please! Please! We beg of you. Where is the Healer?"

The scribes continued arguing with the disciples. Many crowded around to see if anyone could heal the boy.

"There He is!" someone shouted. The crowd ran toward Jesus, Peter, James, and John as they came down off the mountain.

Jesus asked the disciples, "What are you discussing with the scribes?"

The father pushed forward with his son, his wife close behind.

"Teacher, I brought You my son, possessed with a spirit which makes him mute. Whenever it seizes him, it slams him to the ground, and he foams at the mouth. He grinds his teeth and stiffens out. I told Your disciples to cast it out, and they could not do it."[b]

Jesus replied:

"O unbelieving generation, how long shall I be with you? How long shall I put up with you? Bring him to Me."[c]

When the boy saw Jesus, the evil spirit within him threw him into convulsion. He fell to the ground and began rolling around, foaming at the mouth.

Jesus, unphazed, asked the boy's father, "How long has this been happening to him?"

---

a   Mark 5:22-24,35-43
b   Mark 9:17-18 NASB
c   Mark 9:19 NASB

"From childhood. Many times he was thrown into the fire and into the water to destroy him," the father said. "If You can do anything, take pity on us and help us!"

"If I can?" Jesus asked, looking at the father and mother with compassion. "All things are possible to those who believe."

Immediately the boy's father cried out and said, "I do believe!" Jesus looked him in the eyes with compassion, piercing his soul. The father said, "Please help me with my unbelief."

Jesus smiled kindly. He turned to the boy, still on the ground, and commanded, "You deaf and mute spirit, come out of the boy and do not enter him again."

Convulsing and crying out, the boy suddenly became still. People whispered: "He looks like a corpse." "Is he dead?"

Jesus reached down for the boy's hand and raised him. The boy smiled. His parents embraced him.

"Thank You!"

"Thank You!"

The disciples asked Jesus, as they walked to Capernaum, "Why could we not drive out the demon?"

"Because of the littleness of your faith," He said, turning to look them in the eyes. "If you have faith the size of a mustard seed, you will say to this mountain, 'Move from here to there,' and it will move. Nothing will be impossible to you."[a]

Do We Believe?

The boy's father was desperate. He would not take "no" for an answer, but when he asked the Son of God to heal his boy, he

---

a   Matthew 17:19-20

looked in his own heart and realized that he wanted to believe more than he actually believed.

Do we want *to believe that God can heal our world more than we* actually believe *He can?*

Is the same true for us? Are we as desperate to heal the world of the evil of abortion as that father was to heal his son? Do we *want* to believe that God can heal our world more than we *actually believe* He can?

Legal abortion in the United States began 50 years ago in Hawaii, New York, Alaska, and Washington followed by Washington, DC. Then on January 22, 1973, abortion became legal in all 50 states.

Fifty years of legal abortion in the United States: We want legalized abortion to end, but will abortion end when Roe v Wade and Doe v Bolton are overturned? Are we desperate for the end of abortion no matter the laws? Do we believe God can do it?

Check your heart. Do you believe?

Suggested Prayers

Day 2

Mark 11:22-24

Lord, I have faith in You. I believe that You can move the mountain of abortion and that You will use my prayers to do so. I have no doubt in my heart that abortion will be unthinkable in the United States and around the world (name some countries that are on your heart). I pray and ask for the end of abortion. Thank You for granting my request.

Prayer for 40 Days for Life

Lord, thank You for the faithful prayer warriors standing firm for You at abortion facilities around the world. I believe You hear their every prayer, I praise You for ending abortion at those facilities. Thank You for moving the mountain of those abortion facilities into the sea for Your glory.

Day 3

Ephesians 3:20, John 17:21

Lord, You are able to carry out Your purpose and do superabundantly more than all that I dare ask or think, infinitely beyond my greatest prayers, hopes, or dreams, according to Your power that is at work within me. Lord, please increase Your power within me. Open my ears and my faith to hear You more clearly, to be more confident in discerning Your voice over all others.

Prayer for 40 Days for Life

Lord, thank You for carrying out Your purpose and doing superabundantly more than all that the 40 Days for Life prayer warriors dare ask or think, infinitely beyond their greatest prayers, hopes, or dreams, according to Your power that is at work within them. Lord, I stand in the Spirit alongside my sisters and brothers who are praying at abortion facilities. Increase Your power within us as we stand as one in You.

Worship Ahead of the Battle

Jesus, the Way,[a] open my mind to understand the Scriptures.[b]

Worship Warriors

2 Chronicles 20:1-30

"King! King Jehoshaphat! I must speak to the King!"

"What's wrong?"

"The Moabites from the west and Ammonites from the northwest, and even some of the Meunites are readying to attack Judah!"

King Jehoshaphat got word of the impending attack. He muttered to himself, "They're already on the east side of the Dead Sea."

The king remembered that his father, King Asa, had defeated his enemies early in his reign by seeking God before making his

---

a   John 14:6
b   Luke 24:45

battle plan[a] and was rebuked by God later in his life when he devised his own plan rather than seeking God first.[b]

King Jehoshaphat dropped to his knees and prayed, "Oh, Lord, what do we do?"

The King called out to his servants, "A fast! Call all of Judah to fast. We will meet at the temple to seek the Lord!"

The people of Judah, including women and children, traveled to Jerusalem. King Jehoshaphat stood among his people in the court of the temple and prayed:

O Lord, the God of our fathers, are You not God in the heavens? And are You not ruler over all the kingdoms of the nations? Power and might are in Your hand so that no one can stand against You.

Did You not, O our God, drive out the inhabitants of this land before Your people Israel and give it to the descendants of Abraham Your friend forever? They have lived in it, and have built You a sanctuary there for Your name, saying:

> *'Should evil come upon us, the sword, or judgment, or pestilence, or famine, we will stand before this house and before You (for Your name is in this house) and cry to You in our distress, and You will hear and deliver us.'[a]*

Now behold, the sons of Ammon and Moab and Mount Seir, whom You did not let Israel invade when they came out of the land of Egypt (they turned aside from them and did not destroy them), see how they are rewarding us by coming to drive us out from Your possession which You have given us as an inheritance.

---

a   2 Chronicles 14:9-13
b   2 Chronicles 16:7-8
a   King Jehoshaphat was quoting King Solomon's prayer at the dedication of the temple. See 2 Chronicles 6:28-30. God responded to King Solomon with 2 Chronicles 7:14.

O our God, will You not judge them? For we are powerless before this great multitude who are coming against us; nor do we know what to do, but our eyes are on You.[a]

The Holy Spirit came upon Jahaziel, who was a musician among the priestly tribe of Levi, and he said:

Listen, all Judah and the inhabitants of Jerusalem and King Jehoshaphat: thus says the Lord to you, 'Do not fear or be dismayed because of this great multitude, for the battle is not yours but God's.

'Tomorrow go down against them. Behold, they will come up by the ascent of Ziz, and you will find them at the end of the valley in front of the wilderness of Jeruel.

'You need not fight in this battle; station yourselves, stand and see the salvation of the Lord on your behalf, O Judah and Jerusalem.'

'Do not fear or be dismayed; tomorrow go out to face them, for the Lord is with you.'[b]

King Jehoshaphat and all the people fell down prostrate and worshiped ["shachah" in Hebrew] the Lord. Then the priests got up and praised ["halal" in Hebrew] God in a very loud voice.

The next morning, the fighting men of Judah went out to face their enemies. King Jehoshaphat stood and said:

Listen to me, O Judah and inhabitants of Jerusalem, put your trust in the Lord your God and you will be established.[c]

The king consulted with the people and then appointed the musician priests to go out before the army, saying, "Give thanks ["yadah" in Hebrew] to the Lord for His unfailing love is everlasting."

The praise band went ahead of the army singing, "Thank You!" God hadn't even done anything, yet.

---

a   2 Chronicles 20:6-12 NASB
b   2 Chronicles 20:15-17 NASB
c   2 Chronicles 20:20b NASB

When they began singing and praising ["tehillah" in Hebrew], God confused the Ammonites and Moabites so that they fought the inhabitants of Mount Seir and then fought each other.

Not one of the enemies survived.

It took three days for Judah to take the spoil because there was so much! On the fourth day, they assembled and blessed ["barak" in Hebrew] the Lord.

The Jehoshaphat Way

Because all scripture is God-breathed and useful for teaching and training in righteousness so that God's servants may be thoroughly equipped for every good work,[a] let us see what we can learn from Judah's experience during the reign of King Jehoshaphat.

1. King Jehoshaphat sought first God's plan.[b]

2. The people of Judah worshiped God before the battle by:

   - Falling prostrate ["shachah"].
   - Dancing and boasting about God ["halal"].
   - Giving thanks ["yadah"].
   - Singing praise songs ["tehillah"].

3. After God won the battle for them, the people knelt while praising God ["barak"].

---

a   1 Timothy 3:16-17
b   2 Chronicles 20:3

Words for Worship & Praise

shachah (Hebrew)—to fall down flat, prostrate (see 2 Chronicles 20:18, Psalm 29:2)

halal (Hebrew)—base of hallelujah, to boast about the Lord in a kind of foolish way, meaning they were excited, giddy, and probably danced as if no one was looking (see 2 Chronicles 20:19, 21; Psalm 18:3)

yadah (Hebrew)—to give thanks (see 2 Chronicles 20:21; Psalm 7:17)

tehillah (Hebrew)—song or hymn of praise (see 2 Chronicles 20:22; Psalm 22:3)

barak (Hebrew)—to kneel while praising God (see 2 Chronicles 20:26; Psalm 16:7; 18:46)

zamar (Hebrew)—to sing praise, make music (see 1 Chronicles 16:9; Psalm 7:17)

towdah (Hebrew)—confession, thanksgiving (see Psalm 26:7)

latreia (Greek)—service for God (see Romans 12:1; Hebrews 9:1)

Praising God Ahead of Personal Battles

I had been studying this story a few months before I was confronted with a new, yet familiar life test. My brother, who has a mental illness and had been missing for one-and-a-half-years, reappeared. He had disappeared from St. Paul, MN and reappeared in Washington, DC—about an hour from my home.

My brother had shut me out of his life long before this disappearance, so I didn't think he would be willing to see me. However, he was willing to see our mom, who lives with me, so I drove her to Washington, DC several times.

My brother is an avid reader with poor eyesight. He disappeared with his thick glasses and reappeared with none. The hospital said that if we were to take him to get the prescription, he would get new glasses sooner, so I volunteered to take him to get his eyes checked.

My mom did not want to go. The stress of being responsible for him with the possibility of him walking away from us was too much for her.

Mom, Dad, and I talked about the situation at length. None of us was sure how my brother would react to spending several hours with me, but I was not afraid to go. I wanted my brother to have glasses as much as he and my parents, so I made the doctor appointment and arranged my schedule so that I could go.

I left early that morning so that I could find the ophthalmologist's office before I had my brother with me. Traffic in the Washington, DC metro is heavy, like in Atlanta or Los Angeles, so I knew it would be a long day. I got my worship playlist ready before I left home. While driving, I played the music, sang along, and prayed:

"Thy kingdom come. Thy will be done on earth in this very car as it is in heaven. There is peace is heaven so there is peace in this car."

Suddenly, I realized that I was worshiping ahead of a spiritual battle! My attitude changed from concern to confidence. God was going ahead of me to prepare the way—and that He did.

Not only did the day go well, but my brother was smiling and talking to me like a friend by the end of the day. Even my brother's social worker was pleasantly surprised at his good mood. (You'll find the whole story of that day in *ReTested*[a] chapter 12.)

---

a   Cheryl Krichbaum, *ReTested: The Story of a Post-Abortive Woman Called to Change the Conversation* (OH: Author Academy Elite, 2019).

Praising God Ahead of Abortion Battles

As I praised God and marveled over the modern-day connection to an ancient piece of history, the Lord brought my thoughts back to the spiritual warfare of abortion, and I realized that we need to worship ahead of each battle. Abortion battles include but are not limited to:

- A woman considering an abortion or being pressured to abort
- Sex trafficking and women being forced to have abortions by their pimps
- More women choosing abortion because of an economic recession, global pandemic, or natural disaster
- Unfair policing of sidewalk counselors near an abortion facility
- Proposed legislation in committee or sent for vote
- Court cases
- Elections
- Getting balanced news to the people
- Sex education that promotes sex more than education
- Lack of funds for non-profit organizations that support women and families through adoption or parenting

Why Worship?

So often, our prayers overflow with requests rather than praise. Have you ever gathered for prayer and spent most of the time discussing everything that is going wrong? God already knows what we need!

"Your Father knows what you need before you ask Him."
(Matthew 6:8 NASB)

You know Jeremiah 29:11, but do you know verses 12 and 13?

"For I know the plans that I have for you," declares the Lord, "plans for welfare and not for calamity to give you a future and a hope. Then you will call upon Me and come and pray to Me, and I will listen to you. You will seek Me and find Me when you search for Me with all your heart." (Jeremiah 29:11-13 NASB)

As we face each battle, let us have a King Jehoshaphat approach. Rather than run to our own wisdom, let us first seek God.

King Jehoshaphat began his prayer by praising God for what He had done and what He had promised to the people.[a] He quoted King Solomon's words.[b] God had responded to King Solomon's words by saying:

If My people who are called by My name will humble themselves, and pray and seek My face, and turn from their wicked ways, then I will hear from heaven and will forgive their sin and heal their land. (2 Chronicles 7:14 NKJV)

This verse, which we often quote when we talk about revival or refreshing, is an if/then statement: *if* we humble ourselves, pray, seek His face, and turn from our wicked ways, *then* He will hear us, fogive us, and heal our land.

Rather than immediately praying for all the needs that we see, let us first seek His face, His kingdom, and His righteousness.[c]

Behold, the Lord's hand is not so short that it cannot save nor is His ear so dull that it cannot hear. But your iniquities have made a separation between you and your God, and your sins have hidden His face from you so that He does not hear. (Isaiah 59:1-2 NASB)

---

a   2 Chronicles 20:6-9
b   2 Chronicles 20:9, 2 Chronicles 6:28-30
c   Matthew 6:33

Seeking His righteousness means turning from our wicked ways and humbling ourselves.[a] True worship brings us into a position of humbleness and reverence for our all-powerful and all-loving God—the God of justice and the God of agape love. God seeks true worshipers, who worship in spirit and truth.[b]

Let us not be desperate for His hand before we are desperate for His face.

> *Seek first His kingdom and His righteousness, and all these things will be added to you. (Matthew 6:33 NASB)*

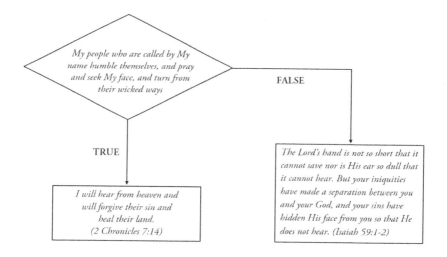

Diagram:

My people who are called by My name humble themselves, and pray and seek My face, and turn from their wicked ways

FALSE

TRUE

I will hear from heaven and will forgive their sin and heal their land. (2 Chronicles 7:14)

The Lord's hand is not so short that it cannot save nor is His ear so dull that it cannot hear. But your iniquities have made a separation between you and your God, and your sins have hidden His face from you so that He does not hear. (Isaiah 59:1-2)

Music & the Brain

Worship changes our focus from our requests to our relationship with God. Although we can worship God in words alone, worshiping God in song is more powerful. Have you noticed that for yourself?

We have thought that music is a right-brain activity, but recent studies have found that music is distributed throughout the

a   2 Chronicles 7:14
b   John 4:24

brain. Nearly every area of the brain is engaged when listening to, composing, playing an instrument, or singing music.[a]

Music itself is powerful. Movies use music to influence how we react to a scene. Elevator music calms us as we travel up and down floors. We use music to cheer ourselves up![b]

When I have felt down, I have turned on Christian music to lift my mood, but what has been even more effective is singing along with the music. Now my first recommendation to my friends who are struggling with difficult situations is to praise God in song even if they don't feel like it.[c]

Worship music is a frequency of love between you and Our Father.

Think of worship music like a frequency of love between you and God. Worship with music to tune into God's frequency of love.

a   Daniel J. Levitin, *This Is Your Brain on Music: The Science of a Human Obsession* (New York: Dutton, 2006), 9.
b   Daniel J. Levitin, *This Is Your Brain on Music: The Science of a Human Obsession* (New York: Dutton, 2006), 9.
c   If there were a thesis in my memoir, *ReTested*, this would be it.

Resources

Your Brain on Music

TEDx Talk by Alan Harvey youtu.be/MZFFwy5fwYI

From Perception to Pleasure: How Music Changes the Brain

TEDx Talk by Dr. Robert Zatorre youtu.be/KVX8j5s53Os

Good Vibrations: The Science of Sound

World Science Festival panelists John Schaefer, Jamshed Bharucha, Christopher Shera, Jacob Kirkegaard, and instrumentalists Polygraph Lounge youtu.be/nsYt-FBhE2Q

Suggested Prayers

Day 4

What's your worship song or hymn for today?_____

What's your posture of worship for today?

☐ dancing/giddying   ☐ prostrating   ☐ giving thanks
☐ praising in song/hymn   ☐ kneeling   ☐ confessing
☐ singing/making music   ☐ serving God

2 Chronicles 20:1-17, 1 John 4:18

Lord, this abortion battle has me fearful, but I seek You and Your love, which casts out all fear.

Lord, do you want me to fast? How do You want me to fast? What do I need to give up so that I can better focus on You and hearing what You have to say?

Oh God, my Lord, are You not Ruler in heaven and do You not rule over all the kingdoms of the nations? In Your hand is power and might so that no one is able to withstand You.

I stand in Your temple of the Spirit and cry out to You in our affliction. Hear and save the babies, their mothers, and all others involved in this murderous attack on our generation. We have no power against this great multitude that is coming against us nor do we know what to do. We can do nothing without You!

Our eyes are upon You. The battle is not ours but Yours. We go out to face the enemy under Your direction. Position us, make us to stand firm and see Your salvation, knowing that You are with us.

Prayer for 40 Days for Life

Lord, encourage my brothers and sisters who are praying at abortion facilities to continually seek You and Your love and not give in to fear.

Thank You for lifting their eyes up to You. Thank You for positioning them while they stand firm, knowing You are with them.

Day 5

What's your worship song or hymn for today?_____

What's your posture of worship for today?

- ☐ dancing/giddying
- ☐ prostrating
- ☐ giving thanks
- ☐ praising in song/hymn
- ☐ kneeling
- ☐ confessing
- ☐ singing/making music
- ☐ serving God

2 Chronicles 20:18-22, 26-30

Lord, I bow my head with my face to the ground before You in worship. I stand and praise You with my voice loud and high! I believe in You, so I can stand firm. I sing to You, praising the beauty of holiness! I praise You for Your mercy endures forever!

Thank You, Lord for setting ambushes against evil, for defeating abortion. Thank You that our enemies wreck one other. When this battle is won, we will assemble and bless You, Lord, with joy with stringed instruments, harps, and trumpets. We trust that reverence for You will increase in all the nations when they hear that You fought against our enemies. We thank You for the rest that is to come when this battle is won.

Prayer for 40 Days for Life

Holy Spirit, prompt the 40 Days for Life prayer warriors to be worship warriors, praising the Lord in song. As they sing and make music, please set ambushes against the evil one, defeating abortion at the very facilities where they sing for joy. Remind them to stand firm in Your name. Deliver them from evil. Thank You for giving them rest.

Days 6–12

Adjust Your Breastplate of Righteousness

J esus, Deliverer,[a] open my mind to understand the Scriptures.[b]

Righteous vs Self-Righteous
Luke 18:9-14

"God, I thank You that I am not like other people: swindlers, the unjust, adulterers, or even like this tax collector," the Pharisee said. "I fast twice a week. I pay tithes of all that I get."

Standing near the back of the sanctuary, the tax collector looks at his feet and said, "God, be merciful to me, the sinner!"

---

a   1 Thessalonians 1:10
b   Luke 24:45

What is Righteousness?

In Jesus' day, tax collectors were considered traitors by the Jews because they worked for the Romans and earned their wages by collecting more than required. They made money off of their people as employees of their oppressors. They had a reputation for being swindlers.

On the surface, the Pharisee appears to be more righteous because he follows all of God's laws religiously, but God is more interested in having a relationship with His humble children.

You may recall the story of Job, who was blameless and upright,[a] yet God allowed satan to test him. Why? Because Job was religious:

> *So it was, when the days of feasting had run their course, that Job would send and sanctify them, and he would rise early in the morning and offer burnt offerings according to the number of them all. For Job said, "It may be that my sons have sinned and cursed God in their hearts." Thus Job did regularly. (Job 1:5 NKJV)*

At the end of Job's story, he had a relationship with God. He didn't just talk to God but heard back from Him. In the end, Job was humble and was a friend of God.

Similarly, the Tax Collector was humble, so Jesus called him "justified":

> *"I tell you, this man went down to his house justified rather than the other [the Pharisee]; for everyone who exalts himself will be humbled, and he who humbles himself will be exalted." (Luke 18:14 NKJV)*

---

a   Job 1:1

Resting in Righteousness

We often think of righteousness as keeping God's commands. God commands us to do certain things and to not do other things. We learn these commands and follow them.

It's the same when we were children. Our parents taught us their rules of what to do and what not to do. We learned their rules and followed them or faced consequences.

Assuming our parents were virtuous, we changed our attitude at some point in our maturity. We had been following our parents' rules because they said so and because we didn't want the consequences of disobedience.

Later, we did things the way our parents taught us to, not out of fear of the consequences, but because we loved them. Then our parents' ways became such a part of us that we do them habitually.

We matured from learning our parents' rules, to following our parents' rules, to behaving well out of respect for our parents, to being the way we are without thinking about our parents' rules.

> *We do things the way our parents taught us not out of fear but because we love them. Then our parents' ways became such a part of us that we do them habitually. The same is tru as children of Our Father.*

God is our perfect parent. We all have varying experiences with our parents, so thinking about God as our parent can bring good feelings or bad. Imagine the best parent you have ever known—your parent, your friend's parent, or even a parent you saw in a TV show. Now, let your imagination go wild about how wonderful that parent is and multiply that wonderfulness by 70 times 7. That's almost as good as God is. But God is an even better parent than that.

Like we mature as children of our earthly parents, we are called to also mature as children of God. We learn what God commands us to do and not to do. We follow those commands, or we don't then face the consequences. As we learn to love and trust God, we change our attitude and follow His commands not out of fear of the consequences but because we love Him. When His ways become a part of us, we just do them without thinking about His commands.

Humbleness

The Pharisee showed himself to be an immature believer by pridefully pointing out his righteousness—that is, he was self-righteous. Jesus says that all who exalt themselves will be humbled, and all who humble themselves will be exalted.[a]

Humbleness is the place to be![b]

Prayers of the Righteous are Effective

If righteousness has become something you strive for, decide today to make righteousness *who* you are. Use the next several days to wash away what you have done that's contrary to God's ways and then let humble righteousness be so ingrained in you that you are at rest. If you sin, get in the habit of confessing it quickly.

Resting in humble righteousness will give you peace in all circumstances. We all want that! Imagine peace in the pandemic, peace during riots, peace during elections. You can have it!

When you have peace in all circumstances, your petitions to the Lord for the end of abortion become more effective.

> *The earnest prayer of a righteous person has great power and produces wonderful results. (James 5:16b NLT)*

Let's Talk About Sex

We cannot talk about abortion without talking about sex. Since we are worshiping for the end of abortion, we must also worship

---

a   Luke 14:11
b   Ephesians 4:2; James 4:6, 10; 1 Peter 5:5; Romans 12:3, 16; Philippians 2:3-4; Matthew 23:12; and of course 2 Chronicles 7:14

for the end of extramarital sex in all its forms. Extramarital sex is sex with someone other than your spouse, including sex before marriage and porn.

It's logical. Women who have abortions are pregnant. Pregnant women had sex with men. If a woman has had extramarital sex, then the man with whom she had sex also had extramarital sex. Therefore, both women and men are responsible for extramarital sex.

Extramarital sex accounts for the majority of abortions. According to the CDC, 86% of American abortions are by unmarried women[a] (one form of extramarital sex). According to Guttmacher Institute, the statistical arm of Planned Parenthood, an estimated 862,320 abortions were provided in abortion facilities in 2017,[b] which is the most recent year of data collection as of the printing of this book. That's 724,349 abortions in 2017 attributed to extramarital sex.

> *Extramarital sex accounts for the majority of abortions—not rape, not incest, not birth defects, not health of the woman.*

In contrast, abortions for other reasons are comparatively low. Guttmacher says that 1% of abortions are the result of rape or

a   Centers for Disease Control and Prevention, "Abortion Surveillance — United States, 2016," *Surveillance Summaries*, November 29, 2019, https://www. cdc.gov/mmwr/volumes/68/ss/ss6811a1.htm.

b   Rachel K. Jones, Elizabeth Witwer, and Jenna Jerman, "Abortion Incidence and Service Availability in the United States, 2017," Guttmacher Institute, 2019, https://www.guttmacher.org/report/ abortion-incidence-service-availability-us-2017#.

incest.[a] Abortion because of health issues of the baby or the mother ranges from 7% to 14%.[b]

Are some abortions by married couples? Yes. Are some abortions for reasons of health by unmarried couples? Yes. Do we know that some abortions are forced by sex traffickers? Yes. There are all sorts of complicating factors, of that there is no doubt. Yet, no matter how you look at the statistics, extramarital sex is one of the biggest factors in the choice to abort.

Even historically, extramarital sex is the major reason abortion became legal. We'll discuss that in more detail in "Day 21" "Consider the Woman at the Well."

Righteousness
What does sex have to do with adjusting our breastplate of righteousness? Simple. We cannot go before God to ask for the end of abortion when we have unconfessed sexual sins.

The Blessing of Sex
Sex is the connection of two people physically, emotionally, and spiritually. Sex is how we make babies. Sex is how the two become one.

From a heavenly perspective, two people who have sex are married and are one flesh. How do we know that? We know from Genesis 2:24, which is before Eve and Adam ate the forbidden fruit:

a   Lawrence B. Finer, Lori F. Frohwirth, Lindsay A. Dauphinee, Susheela Singh and Ann M. Moore, "Reasons U.S. Women Have Abortions: Quantitative and Qualitative Perspectives," *Perspectives on Sexual and Reproductive Health* 37, no. 3 (2005): 110–118 https://www.guttmacher.org/sites/default/files/pdfs/pubs/psrh/full/3711005.pdf

b   Guttmacher Institute. "Reasons U.S. Women Have Abortions: Quantitative and Qualitative Perspectives." guttmacher.org/journals/psrh/2005/reasons-us-women-have-abortions-quantitative-and-qualitative-perspectives accessed August 2018.

Jaime L. Natoli, Deborah L. Ackerman, Suzanne McDermott, and Janice G. Edwards and published with the title of "Prenatal diagnosis of Down syndrome: a systematic review of termination rates (1995–2011)," March 14, 2012: obgyn.onlinelibrary.wiley.com/doi/full/10.1002/pd.2910 accessed October 2018.

Therefore, a man shall leave his father and mother and be joined to his wife, and they shall become one flesh.

Jesus quotes Genesis 2:24:

And He [Jesus] answered and said to them, "Have you not read that He who made them at the beginning 'made them male and female," and said,

> *'For this reason, a man shall leave his father and mother and be joined to his wife, and the two shall become one flesh*[b]*?*

So then, they are no longer two but one flesh. Therefore, what God has joined together, let not man separate." (Matt 19:4-6)

God created sex to bring us back together as one. Adam was one and then became two.[c] Just two-to-three verses later, God declared that when husband and wife are joined, they become one flesh.[d] The Apostle Paul calls the husband-wife relationship a profound mystery and compares it to Christ's relationship to The Church.[e]

God created sex to make more people!

God created sex to benefit our bodies. Studies show that sex improves our heart health, reduces our blood pressure, and boosts our immune system.[f]

---

a   Genesis 1:27
b   Genesis 2:24
c   Genesis 2:21-22
d   Genesis 2:24
e   Ephesians 5:32
f   "Center for Women's Health." OHSU. Accessed August 29, 2020. https://www.ohsu.edu/womens-health/benefits-healthy-sex-life
Galan, Nicole. "Health Benefits of Sex: Research, Findings, and Cautions." Medical News Today. August 23, 2019. Accessed August 29, 2020. https://www.medicalnewstoday.com/articles/316954.
Rogers, Pamela, and Ana Gotter. "The Health Benefits of Sex." Healthline. October 18, 2018. Accessed August 29, 2020. https://www.healthline.com/health/healthy-sex-health-benefits.

Sexual Immorality

In 1 Corinthians 6:13, the Apostle Paul explains that our bodies are not for sexual immorality but for the Lord, and the Lord is for our bodies. He explains that when we join with someone who is prostituting his or her body, we become one with him or her for the two shall become one flesh,[a] again quoting Genesis 2:24. Paul is saying that we are one with whomever we have sex, even if that person is not our spouse.

Paul says that we should flee sexual immorality—that is, do an about face and run away!—because every other sin is outside the body, but extramarital sex is against our own bodies. We are to glorify God with our bodies.[b]

As you likely know, sexual immorality does not benefit our bodies because it puts us at risk for sexually transmitted infections (STIs), which may become sexually transmitted diseases (STDs). With every partner, our likelihood to get at least one STI increases exponentially. Not only do STIs make us uncomfortable, produce ugly-looking sores on our private parts, and decrease our immune system's ability to protect us, but STDs can decrease our ability to procreate.[c]

Temple of the Holy Spirit

Paul says something even more profound. He says that our bodies are the temple of the Holy Spirit.[d] What does that mean? Remember that the Jews went to the temple to worship God. Before the Jewish temple was torn down by the Romans, God resided in the temple.

The pagans in Paul's time had similar practices. They went to temples to worship their gods. The temple of Aphrodite was in

---

a   1 Corinthians 6:15-16

b   1 Corinthians 6:18, 20

c   I honestly wrote all that from memory because it's in *The Missing Sex Ed Lessons* online courses!

d   1 Corinthians 6:19

Corinth. The temple of Artemus, one of the seven wonders of the ancient world, was in Ephesus.

In contrast, as Christians we worship God from within ourselves. Because the Holy Spirit resides in us, our bodies are temples of the Holy Spirit.

Of course, you can go to a church building to worship God, and by no means am I suggesting that you stop assembling:

> Let us consider how to stimulate one another to love and good deeds, not forsaking our own assembling together, as is the habit of some, but encouraging one another. (Hebrews 10:24-25a NASB)

You can also go to a Christian concert to worship God.

But you can—and should—worship God from within yourself no matter where you are and no matter what day of the week. You are free to worship God anytime and all the time, and you are encouraged to do so:

> [Jesus said,] "But an hour is coming, and now is, when the true worshipers will worship the Father in spirit and truth; for such people the Father seeks to be His worshipers." (John 4:23 NASB)

Wash Clean

Just like you would not defile your church building, you should also not defile your own temple of the Holy Spirit.

If someone were to vandalize your church building, you would go clean up the mess. In the same way, if you have defiled your temple of the Holy Spirit, spend time washing it clean, making it white as snow.[a]

Be careful that you do not get too focused on technicalities. God knows the truth, so don't try to tell Him half truths. If you have

a   Psalm 51:7, Isaiah 1:18

done any of the following, confess it. (Trust that I, too, have confessed my sexual sins.)

- Oral, anal, or vaginal sex with anyone other than your legal spouse
- Sex with someone who is of the same gender as you
- Pornography[a] and lust
- Addiction to masturbation[b]

—⁂—

Today's Pharisee

Today, Jesus' parable might look like this:

"God, I thank You that I am not like other people: abortionists, women who abort, women who hookup with just anyone. Such sluts," said the Pharisaical Christian. "I only had sex with a few people before my spouse. I only look at a little porn, but it doesn't affect my marriage. I go to church twice a week. I pay tithes of all that I get. I even volunteer."

On her knees, the post-abortive woman bows her head and says, "Lord, my Savior, please forgive me for having sex outside of marriage and for murdering my daughter. I miss her. I'm so sorry. Thank You for taking care of her in heaven. I want to name my daughter. Would that be okay? It seems strange to ask. I'm her mother, but I murdered her! Forgive me, Lord, and tell me what You want me to name my baby."

---

a *Sexual immorality* is translated from the Greek word *porneia*, from which we get the word *pornography*.

b Although the Bible does not address masturbation specifically, we know from neuroscience that masturbation is sex and that sex neurochemically bonds us with other people, and we know from the Bible that we are only to have sex with our spouse. You can learn more about the neuroscience of sex in *The Missing Sex Ed Lessons*.

The abortion-minded feel like they are being lectured by Pharisees. Let's prove them wrong.

"By this all will know that you are My disciples, if you have [agape] love for one another." (John 13:35 NKJV)

Resources

Bible Verses on Sexual Immorality

Both the Old and New Testaments have a lot to say about sex. Are we Christians ignorant of what God deems important? Read what is recorded in the Bible. MybodyMyworship.com/bible-verses-on-sexual-immorality.html

The Missing Sex Ed Lessons

Faith- and science-based courses that equip tweens, teens, and unmarried adults to delay sexual encounters so that they avoid STIs, crisis pregnancies, and challenging relationships. These online courses provide positive, empowering, pro-life sex education completed in the privacy of your own home. MybodyMyworship.com

Suggested Prayers

Satan does not want you cleansed of all unrighteousness, so don't be surprised if he attacks you. He is a thief and a liar. After each one of these prayers, consider returning to *Day 1* to pray the Armor of God (on page 6) and increasing your worship music. Sing through all circumstances!

Day 6

What's your worship song or hymn for today?_____

What's your posture of worship for today?

☐ dancing/giddying   ☐ prostrating   ☐ giving thanks
☐ praising in song/hymn   ☐ kneeling   ☐ confessing
☐ singing/making music   ☐ serving God

James 5:16; Psalm 46:10, 139:23-24; 1 John 1:8-10

Lord, my Redeemer,[a] the prayers of the righteous can accomplish much. I seek righteousness not through striving but through confessing my sins. If I say I have no sin, I deceive myself and the truth is not in me. If I confess my sin, You are faithful and just to forgive me and cleanse me from all unrighteousness. I will not make You a liar by saying that I have not sinned. Your word is in me. Search me and know me, oh God. Bring to light what I need to confess. (Confess whatever He brings to mind.)

Lord, I trust the blood of Your sacrifice on the cross to cleanse me of all unrighteousness. (Imagine yourself being washed clean.)

Prayer for 40 Days for Life

Jesus, our Advocate,[b] I stand firm with my sisters and brothers who are praying at abortion facilities around the world today.

---

a   Psalm 19:14
b   1 John 2:1

Wash them, too, of all their sins so that their breastplates protect their vital organs.

(Suggested: Pray Day 1 Armor of God on page 6.)

Day 7

What's your worship song or hymn for today?_____

What's your posture of worship for today?

- ☐ dancing/giddying
- ☐ prostrating
- ☐ giving thanks
- ☐ praising in song/hymn
- ☐ kneeling
- ☐ confessing
- ☐ singing/making music
- ☐ serving God

Psalm 32:3-5

Lord, my just Judge,[a] when I refused to confess my sin, my body felt weak, and I groaned all day long. Day and night your hand of discipline was upon me. My strength evaporated like water in the summer heat. Finally, I confessed my sins to You. I do that again today.

Lord, research explains that sex, even fantasies of sex, bonds us with other people or fantasies of other people.[b] Therefore, I confess all my sexual sins, including _____, _____, and _____, no longer trying to hide my guilt from You. I confess my rebellion to You, Lord.

Jesus, I ask that the blood of Your sacrifice on the cross break the bonds that I created with anyone and everyone other than my spouse.

Thank you for forgiving me! My guilt is gone!

---

a   Psalm 7:11
b   See The Missing Sex Ed Lessons at MybodyMyworship.com to learn more research on extramarital sex and righteous sex.

Prayer for 40 Days for Life

Lord, thank You for forgiving the sins of those praying and counseling at abortion facilities around the world.

(Suggested: Pray *Day* 1 Armor of God on page 6.)

Day 8

What's your worship song or hymn for today?_____

What's your posture of worship for today?

- ☐ dancing/giddying
- ☐ prostrating
- ☐ giving thanks
- ☐ praising in song/hymn
- ☐ kneeling
- ☐ confessing
- ☐ singing/making music
- ☐ serving God

James 4:7-10, 2 Chronicles 7:14

Lord, I agree to do things Your way. I choose to humble myself, to turn from the world's ways, and to seek Your face, not just what I want You to give me.

I resist the devil so that he will flee from me. I choose to draw near to You through worship, prayer, and Bible study, and I trust that You will draw near to me. I cleanse my hands and purify my heart. I grieve, mourn, and weep over my sins. I humble myself in Your sight, trusting that You will lift me up.

Prayer for 40 Days for Life

Lord, thank You for the sidewalk counselors who choose to humble themselves and to seek Your face. Thank You for drawing near to them and lifting them up.

(Suggested: Pray *Day* 1 Armor of God on page 6.)

Day 9

What's your worship song or hymn for today?_____

What's your posture of worship for today?

- ☐ dancing/giddying
- ☐ prostrating
- ☐ giving thanks
- ☐ praising in song/hymn
- ☐ kneeling
- ☐ confessing
- ☐ singing/making music
- ☐ serving God

1 Corinthians 6:9-13, 18-19

Lord, we know that the unrighteous will not inherit Your kingdom. Do not let The Church be deceived; neither fornicators, nor idolaters, nor adulterers, nor male prostitutes, nor homosexuals, nor thieves, nor the covetous, nor drunkards, nor revilers, nor swindlers will inherit Your kingdom.

Such were some of us, but we were washed, but we were sanctified, but we were justified in the name of the Lord Jesus Christ and in the Holy Spirit.

All things are lawful for me, but not all things are profitable. All things are lawful for me, but I will not be mastered by anything. Yet the body is not for sexual immorality, but for You, and You are for the body.

I choose daily to flee sexual immorality. Soften the hearts of all The Church to flee sexual immorality for every other sin is outside the body, but the sexually immoral person sins against his or her own body.

Prayer for 40 Days for Life

Lord, thank You for sanctifying and justifying the 40 Days for Life prayer warriors in the name of Jesus Christ and in the Holy Spirit.

Day 10

What's your worship song or hymn for today?_____

What's your posture of worship for today?

- ☐ dancing/giddying
- ☐ prostrating
- ☐ giving thanks
- ☐ praising in song/hymn
- ☐ kneeling
- ☐ confessing
- ☐ singing/making music
- ☐ serving God

1 Corinthians 6:9-11, Psalm 139:23-24, Galatians 5:13

Lord, I realize that those who do wrong will not inherit Your Kingdom; therefore, I will do what's right in Your eyes not for fear of consequences but out of love for You.

I will not indulge in sexual sin (look lustfully, look at porn, or have any sex outside of marriage), worship idols (not even coffee or wine), steal, be greedy, get drunk, be abusive, or cheat others. I was called to freedom, and I will not turn my freedom into an opportunity for my flesh but instead, through love, serve others.

Search me and know my heart, Lord. If there is any sin within me, bring it to my mind so that I can confess it. Wake me in the night if You have to. Let no sin prevent me from being righteous in Your eyes.

Thank You, Lord, that I am no longer a stranger but instead one of Your children, an heir to Your Kingdom. Thank You for cleansing me, making me holy, and making me right with You through Your Holy Spirit and through my calling on the name of the Lord Jesus Christ.

Prayer for 40 Days for Life

Lord, search the hearts of the sidewalk counselors and bring to their minds their sins so that they can confess them. Let no sin prevent them from being righteous in Your eyes. Thank You that they are also Your children and therefore my sisters and brothers. Thank You for cleansing our family, making us holy and right with You through Your Holy Spirit and through our calling on the name of Jesus. Through love, we serve one another for Your glory, not our own.

(Suggested: Pray Day 1 Armor of God on page 6.)

Day 11

What's your worship song or hymn for today?_____

What's your posture of worship for today?

- ☐ dancing/giddying
- ☐ prostrating
- ☐ giving thanks
- ☐ praising in song/hymn
- ☐ kneeling
- ☐ confessing
- ☐ singing/making music
- ☐ serving God

Romans 12:1, Psalm 66:18-20

Lord, I give You my body because of all You have done for me. My body is a living and holy sacrifice, the kind You find acceptable. This is my true worship of You. It's my body and with it I choose to worship You.

Lord, if I had not confessed the sin in my heart, You would not have listened, but You did listen! You pay attention to my prayers. Praise You, who does not ignore my prayers or withdraw Your unfailing love for me. I know that the prayers of the righteous are powerful, and I thank You for making my prayers powerful now that I am right with You.

Prayer for 40 Days for Life

Lord, I praise You for listening to the prayers of the 40 Days for Life worship warriors. Thank You for Your unfailing love for them and the women and men they counsel. Thank You for answering their powerful prayers because doing so brings You glory.

(Suggested: Pray Day 1 Armor of God on page 6.)

Day 12

What's your worship song or hymn for today?_____

What's your posture of worship for today?

☐ dancing/giddying   ☐ prostrating   ☐ giving thanks
☐ praising in song/hymn   ☐ kneeling   ☐ confessing
☐ singing/making music   ☐ serving God

1 Thessalonians 4:1-8, James 4:7

Lord, thank You for instructing me on how to live in order to please You. Thank You that I am living in Your will more and more and influencing others to do the same by my example, by the service You call me to do, and by the words You provide me to say.

Thank You for sanctifying me. Thank You for protecting me from all temptations of sexual immorality, including pornography. Thank You for Your still, small voice that gently reminds me to control my own body in a way that is holy and honorable, not in passionate lust like those who do not know You. I resist the devil so he must flee from me. Thank You for calling me to live a holy life, which benefits my health and my relationships.

Prayer for 40 Days for Life

Lord, thank You that the sidewalk counselors are living in Your will and lovingly influencing others to do the same. Thank You for their service to You. Thank You for providing them with words to say to all with whom they interact.

Thank You for sanctifying the sidewalk counselors and protecting them from all temptations, reminding them to flee from the devil.

(Suggested: Pray Day 1 Armor of God on page 6.)

DAYS 13–17

Forgive &
Be Set Free

J esus, my Judge,[a] open my mind to understand the Scriptures.[b]

The Disciples Prayer
Matthew 6:6-15, Matthew 18:23-35

In the Sermon on the Mount, Jesus said:

"When you pray, you are not to be like the hypocrites; for they love to stand and pray in the synagogues and on the street corners so that they may be seen by men. Truly I say to you, they have their reward in full.

"But you, when you pray, go into your inner room, close your door and pray to your Father who is in secret, and your Father who sees what is done in secret will reward you.

---

a   Acts 10:42
b   Luke 24:45

"And when you are praying, do not use meaningless repetition as the Gentiles do, for they suppose that they will be heard for their many words. So do not be like them; for your Father knows what you need before you ask Him.

"Pray, then, in this way:

'Our Father who is in heaven, hallowed be Your name.

'Your kingdom come. Your will be done, on earth as it is in heaven.

'Give us this day our daily bread.

'And forgive us our debts, as we also have forgiven our debtors.

'And do not lead us into temptation but deliver us from evil.'

"For if you forgive others for their transgressions, your heavenly Father will also forgive you. But if you do not forgive others, then your Father will not forgive your transgressions."

The Profound Mystery of Forgiveness

You may have grown up in a church or now attend a church that says this prayer so often that you have it memorized. Memorizing scripture is wonderful because you can use it when you need to. As I described in "Days 4-5" "Worship Ahead of the Battle" and even more so in *ReTested*, I have prayed "Your kingdom come. Your will be done, on earth as it is in heaven" with amazing results.

What bothers me, though, is that for decades, I didn't think about what those words in the prayer meant. I only parroted them in church.

Further, I never stopped to think what my debts (or trespasses or sins) were, I never truly asked for forgiveness, and I certainly didn't think about whom I needed to forgive.

Additionally, I completely missed that this prayer—and Jesus' explanation after it—points out a profound connection between forgiving others and receiving forgiveness from God.

We can ask for forgiveness all day, but we are hypocrites when we ask for forgiveness yet won't forgive others.

Jesus explained with this parable:

> *"The kingdom of heaven is like a certain king who wanted to settle accounts with his servants. And when he had begun to settle accounts, one was brought to him who owed him ten thousand talents. But as he was not able to pay, his master commanded that he be sold, with his wife and children and all that he had, and that payment be made.*
>
> *"The servant therefore fell down before him, saying, 'Master, have patience with me, and I will pay you all.' Then the master of that servant was moved with compassion, released him, and forgave him the debt.*
>
> *"But that servant went out and found one of his fellow servants who owed him a hundred denarii; and he laid hands on him and took him by the throat, saying, 'Pay me what you owe!'*
>
> *"So his fellow servant fell down at his feet and begged him, saying, 'Have patience with me, and I will pay you all.' And he would not but went and threw him into prison till he should pay the debt.*
>
> *"So when his fellow servants saw what had been done, they were very grieved, and came and told their master all that had been done.*

"Then his master, after he had called him, said to him, 'You wicked servant! I forgave you all that debt because you begged me. Should you not also have had compassion on your fellow servant, just as I had pity on you?' And his master was angry and delivered him to the torturers until he should pay all that was due to him.

"So My heavenly Father also will do to you if each of you, from his heart, does not forgive his brother his trespasses." (Matthew 18:23-35 NKJV)

This parable was Jesus' answer to Peter's question: "How often do I have to forgive another when he continually sins against me? Seven times?"

Jesus answered, "Not just seven times but 70 times seven."

Someone who is hard-hearted might keep a tally sheet of how many times they have forgiven someone and stop at 490 times, but a humble person will forgive all the way to death (from the cross, Jesus said, "Forgive them, Father, for they know not what they do"[a]).

Just as confession returns us to righteousness, so does forgiveness. Unforgiveness weighs us down, but forgiveness frees us of the weight of debt.

"Forgive us our debts as we have forgiven others." (Matthew 6:12)

In *ReTested*, I tell the story of how forgiving others replaced my bitterness with joy. But something more happened that I didn't share in my memoir.

I had not been feeling rested even though I was sleeping through the night. My back was tight. I was going to the chiropractor twice a week, which made my back feel better for a day or two, but it wouldn't hold. I began stretching my back every night before

---

a   Luke 23:34

bed, but I still felt tight again every morning, so I stretched my back again.

At that time, I was in the post-abortion healing class feeling bitter, but I didn't think my bitterness was from my abortion. Although I felt completely healed from my abortion, I knew that I was still upset by all the things that led to having sex outside of marriage in the first place. I wanted to get rid of my bitterness so badly that I sought the Lord. He brought me to Ephesians 4:31-32, which says:

> *Let all bitterness and wrath and anger and clamor and slander be put away from you, along with all malice. Be kind to one another, tenderhearted,* forgiving each other, *just as God in Christ also has forgiven you. [emphasis mine]*

I spent an afternoon with God, seeking to get rid of my bitterness. I wanted to feel joy, not bitterness, so I asked the Lord to bring to my mind anyone with whom I was angry.

One by one, I prayed through each source of bitterness and forgave each person I held responsible for whatever went wrong. I spent a

I wanted to feel joy, not bitterness

whole afternoon just forgiving people. Among them were all the Christians who didn't seem to welcome me after I gave my testimony.

Then I thought about every story of bitterness I had ever heard from my parents and my grandparents. I realized I had agreed with their bitterness, so I identified the people whom I blamed for each instance, and I forgave them. I even forgave my pastor grandfather, who died 40 years before, for not teaching my mom to study the bible or pray at home. Then I realized that his parents hadn't taught him to study and pray at home and neither did his seminary, so I forgave all of them, too.

I wanted my joy back so badly that every time I forgave someone, I asked the Lord to replace the space that bitterness had left with joy. By the end of the afternoon, I felt lighter!

Although I felt like I had thought of everything and everyone against whom I had harbored bitterness, I wanted to make sure I was completely clean of unforgiveness. I asked the Lord again to reveal to me any root of bitterness.

> *Search me, O God... and see if there be any hurtful way in me and lead me in the everlasting way. (Psalm 139:23a, 24 NASB)*

Before bed, I prayed that the Lord would teach me in the night. A few days later, I woke up at 5 am from a dream in which I was really mad at my husband. I didn't want to be awake, but the Lord whispered to me to go pray. I was going to sit in the recliner when I felt Him tell me to kneel. I probably would have fallen asleep in the recliner, but I wouldn't fall asleep on my knees.

> *I wanted my joy back so badly that every time I forgave someone, I asked the Lord to replace the my bitterness with joy.*

I forgave my husband. Back to bed I went and slept for another three hours! When I woke up, I couldn't remember why I had been angry in the dream, and I still don't remember today.

Not only did I wake up free from my bitterness, but I was free from my sore back. I didn't need to stretch because my back felt great! I literally felt free from the heaviness of my bitterness.

Forgiveness isn't about the other person. I did not go to my husband and say, "I forgive you." Instead I went to God and said, "I forgive him."

Whether my husband feels sorry for what he did is not the point. Whether *I* feel sorry for harboring bitterness toward him *is* the point.

Suggested Prayers

Day 13

What's your worship song or hymn for today?_____

What's your posture of worship for today?

☐ dancing/giddying   ☐ prostrating   ☐ giving thanks
☐ praising in song/hymn ☐ kneeling   ☐ confessing
☐ singing/making music   ☐ serving God

Matthew 6:12, 14-15, Mark 11:25; Psalm 139:23-24; Ephesians 6:14

Lord, You said that I must forgive anyone I am holding a grudge against so that You will forgive my sins, too. In what we call The Lord's Prayer, we ask You to forgive us our sins as we have forgiven those who sin against us.

Lord, forgiving others is scary to me. It feels like I am saying that what the other person did is okay. It's not okay! But I trust You, Lord, to work in the hearts of all people to bring repentance in their own hearts so that they, too, will be closer to You.

Because I trust You, I take this time now to forgive _____ for _____. Thank You for blessing _____ and for forgiving me, too.

Lord, please show me who I refuse to forgive. Who else, Lord? Lord, I will list every grievance, every complaint, every bitterness and forgive whomever I hold responsible—even if I'm mad at You!

Lord, I thank You for showing me with whom I am angry so that I can release myself from the chains of bitterness and rejoice in being closer to You.

Lord, search me thoroughly and know my heart. Test me and know my anxious thoughts. See if there is any wicked or hurtful way in me. Lead me in the everlasting way. Remind me to confess my sins quickly throughout every day so that the breastplate of righteousness will easily slide back into place, protecting all my vital organs.

Prayer for 40 Days for Life

Lord, thank You for reminding the 40 Days for Life worship warriors of the meanings behind the words of the Lord's Prayer. May they forgive quickly every offense and rejoice in their closeness to You.

(Suggested: Pray *Day* 1 Armor of God on page 6.)

Day 14

What's your worship song or hymn for today?_____

What's your posture of worship for today?
- ☐ dancing/giddying
- ☐ praising in song/hymn
- ☐ singing/making music
- ☐ prostrating
- ☐ kneeling
- ☐ serving God
- ☐ giving thanks
- ☐ confessing

Luke 23:34-37, Ephesians 4:31-32, Psalm 32:4, Galatians 5:22-23, Colossians 4:6

Lord, most of the women and men choosing abortion know not what they do. They do not see the evil. They sincerely believe that abortion is the better choice for their situation for they fear the world more than they trust Your love.

Lord, my heart breaks that they don't see as we see. My heart breaks that their vitality drains away, that they become numb to life. Yet I choose to forgive them. Lord, forgive them for they know not what they do.

Lord, I choose to be tenderhearted to hurting women and scared men and to let go of all bitterness, wrath, anger, clamor, malice, and evil speaking toward the abortion-minded, the pro-choice, the pro-abortion, and the post-abortive. Instead, I choose to be kind to all others and forgiving, as You forgave me. Let my speech always be with grace, seasoned with salt, that I may know how I ought to answer each one.

Prayer for 40 Days for Life

Lord, protect the tender hearts of the sidewalk counselors. Thank You for their hearts for hurting women and scared men. Thank You for their love, joy, peace, patience, kindness, goodness, faithfulness, gentleness, and self-control. Give them words filled with grace, seasoned with salt so that they may know how they ought to answer each person who opposes You through them.

(Suggested: Pray *Day* 1 Armor of God on page 6.)

Day 15

What's your worship song or hymn for today?_____

What's your posture of worship for today?

- ☐ dancing/giddying
- ☐ prostrating
- ☐ giving thanks
- ☐ praising in song/hymn
- ☐ kneeling
- ☐ confessing
- ☐ singing/making music
- ☐ serving God

Luke 11:13, Galatians 5:22-23, Proverbs 18:10

Lord, now that I have cleansed myself of sin and unforgiveness, replace those cleaned out spaces of my heart with more of the Holy Spirit. Let the fruit of the Spirit be evident in me today and every day: love, joy, peace, patience, kindness, goodness, faithfulness, gentleness, and self-control.

Thank You, Lord, that Your name is a strong tower. Thank You that in my righteousness, I can run into the strong tower of Your name and be safe.

Prayer for 40 Days for Life

Lord, thank You for giving sidewalk counselors more of the Holy Spirit so that they have more fruit of the Spirit: love, joy, peace, patience, kindness, goodness, faithfulness, gentleness, and self-control. Thank You for being their strong tower, protecting them during this battle.

(Suggested: Pray *Day* 1 Armor of God on page 6.)

Day 16

What's your worship song or hymn for today?_____

What's your posture of worship for today?
- ☐ dancing/giddying
- ☐ prostrating
- ☐ giving thanks
- ☐ praising in song/hymn
- ☐ kneeling
- ☐ confessing
- ☐ singing/making music
- ☐ serving God

James 4:3, 5:16

Lord, let my every request be made from love and not self-righteousness. Remind me to ask rightly for Your glory and not for my passions. I know full well that the prayers of the righteous are powerful and effective. Am I as righteous as I can be? Is there anything left for me to confess or anyone left to forgive so that I may realize the closeness to You that righteousness grants?

(If you are angry with men, take this time to forgive them. If you are angry with women, take this time to forgive them. If you are angry at The Church, take this time to forgive her. If you are angry at the government or politicians, take this time to forgive them. If you are angry at racists, take this time to forgive them.)

Lord, encourage me by showing me just how powerful and effective my prayers are—for Your glory, not my own.

Prayer for 40 Days for Life

Lord, thank You for showing the 40 Days for Life worship warriors just how powerful and effective their prayers are.

(Suggested: Pray *Day* 1 Armor of God on page 6.)

Day 17

What's your worship song or hymn for today?_____

What's your posture of worship for today?

☐ dancing/giddying   ☐ prostrating   ☐ giving thanks
☐ praising in song/hymn   ☐ kneeling   ☐ confessing
☐ singing/making music   ☐ serving God

2 Corinthians 5:14-20, Joel 2:25

Lord, it's Your love that fuels my passion and motivates me because I am absolutely convinced that You gave Your life for all. Because of You, I no longer live a self-absorbed life but instead pour out myself for You.

Thank You for giving me a new perspective that refuses to evaluate people by their outward appearances. Thank You for reconciling me to You! Thank You for using me to reach others so that they may choose to reconcile with You, too. I am a new creation because of You. May the abortion-minded become new creations, too! Thank You for redeeming the years that the swarming locust has eaten.

Prayer for 40 Days for Life

Thank You for using sidewalk counselors to reach women and men in crisis so that they may choose to reconcile with You.

(Suggested: Pray Day 1 Armor of God on page 6.)

Interlude

Who Are You?

J esus, the true vine,[a] open my mind to understand the scriptures.[b]

Be the Branch
John 15:1-11, 10:10

"I am the true vine," Jesus said. "You are the branches. Our Father is the vinedresser.

"Branches cannot bear fruit unless they remain in the vine, for apart from Me you can do nothing.

"Our Father prunes every branch that bears fruit so that it may bear more fruit.

"If you remain in Me and My commands remain in you, ask whatever you wish, and it will be done for you.

"When you bear much fruit, you glorify Our Father and show yourself to be My disciple.

"I tell you this so that My joy may be in you and that your joy may be full, for I came that you may have life and have it abundantly."

---

a   John 15:1
b   Luke 24:45

After completing Days 6-17 "Adjust Your Breastplate of Righteousness" and "Forgive & Be Set Free" are you feeling like a pruned branch?

After pruning, branches are lighter. Do you feel lighter?

When you are pruned through confession and forgiveness, you make room for spiritual things to grow. When you prayed to forgive others, which fruit of the Spirit did you most want God to grow?

☐ love   ☐ joy   ☐ peace
☐ patience   ☐ kindness   ☐ goodness
☐ faithfulness   ☐ gentleness   ☐ self-control

I am praying that you are refreshed and feeling the joy of the Lord!

I encourage you to return to the *Day* 1 Armor of God prayer on page 6 so that you protect yourself from being weighed down again by the lies of the enemy.

As you continue through this book, stand firm in Christ, remembering who you are in Christ:

- Chosen[a]

- God's creation[b]

- Made in God's image[c]

- Holy and royal priesthood[d]

- Holy nation[e]

---

a   John 15:16, 1 Thessalonians 1:4, 1 Peter 2:9
b   Genesis 1:26-27; 2; Psalm 139:13-14
c   Genesis 1:26-27
d   1 Peter 2:5, 9
e   1 Peter 2:9

- People for God[a]
- Living stones[b]
- Son, child, heir[c]
- Appointed[d]
- The Temple of the Holy Spirit[e]

I encourage you to stand firm and be:

- Holy[f]
- One with Him[g]
- A living sacrifice[h]

Keep yourself in Christ. Imagine yourself as Solomon's beautiful temple and the Holy Spirit living inside of you. From this beautiful temple—*that's you!*—worship Him and ask in His name.

---

a   1 Peter 2:10
b   1 Peter 2:5
c   Romans 8:15-17, Ephesians 1:18, James 2:5, John 1:12-13
d   John 15:16
e   1 Corinthians 6:19, 2 Corinthians 6:16
f   1 Peter 1:15-16, 2:9-10; Romans 12:1-2; Ephesians 1:3b-4
g   John 17:21, 23
h   Romans 12:1-2

Suggested Prayers

Day 18

What's your worship song or hymn for today?_____

What's your posture of worship for today?

☐ dancing/giddying   ☐ prostrating   ☐ giving thanks
☐ praising in song/hymn   ☐ kneeling   ☐ confessing
☐ singing/making music   ☐ serving God

Genesis 1:26-27, 1 Corinthians 6:19, 2 Corinthians 6:16, 1 Peter 2:9, Romans 12:1-2, Romans 8:15-17, Ephesians 1:18, James 2:5, John 1:12-13, John 17:21, 23, John 15:5, 1 Peter 1:5-8

Lord, thank You for making me in Your image. Thank You for creating my beautiful temple. Lord, I honor Your creation by believing that You made me beautiful. I stand firm as Your royal priesthood, as a living sacrifice, as Your child, as Your heir. I choose holiness and oneness with You, remaining in the True Vine.

With diligence, I add moral excellence to my faith. To my moral excellence, I add understanding. To my understanding, I add the strength of self-control. To my self-control, I add perseverance. To my perseverance, I add godliness. To my godliness, I add mercy. To mercy, I add unending agape love.

Prayer for 40 Days for Life

Lord, thank You for showing the beauty of Your creation to the 40 Days for Life prayer warriors—the beauty in the babies, the beauty in their mothers, the beauty in those supporting or pressuring the mothers, the beauty in the abortion workers, and the beauty in the police. Give them self-control, perseverance, mercy, and unending agape love.

History Lessons

Day 19

Remember the Man Caught in Adultery

J esus, He who brings justice,[a] open my mind to understand the Scriptures.[b]

Humiliated

John 8:1-11

Early in the morning, Jesus went to the temple. People began crowding around Him in the Temple court, and He began to teach them.

A commotion interrupted Jesus' teaching. The crowd turned to see scribes and Pharisees pulling a woman with disheveled hair into the court. "Let go of me! Leave me alone!" Then she saw Jesus and stood quietly, ashamed. Jesus looked at the woman's face with compassion, but she would not look up.

A Pharisee said, "Teacher, this woman has been caught in adultery, in the very act."

a   Luke 18:7-8, John 8:10-11
b   Luke 24:45

Another said, "In the Law, Moses commanded us to stone such women. What then do You say?" The scribes and Pharisees were testing Jesus so that they might have grounds for accusing Him.[a]

The scribes and Pharisees were referring to Leviticus 20:10 and Deuteronomy 22:22, which say that both "the adulterer and the adulteress shall surely be put to death." Jesus knew The Law, so He knew the adulterer was missing from this accusation.

Yet He doesn't say a word. Instead, He draws their attention away from the woman's nakedness and down to the ground. Perhaps Jesus gave a knowing look to the 12 who quietly covered the woman's nakedness. Everyone got closer to see what He was writing in the sand. Someone near Jesus read His words out loud, and one-by-one the woman's accusers—the older ones first—walked away from the woman, who was in the center of the court. They didn't leave the crowd, of course, because they wanted to see what Jesus would do.

What did He write in the sand? We don't know. Perhaps He quoted scripture.[b]

Jesus straightened up, looked the woman in the eye, and said, "Woman, where are they? Did no one condemn you?"

She said, "No one, Lord."

And Jesus said, "I do not condemn you, either. Go and sin no more."[c]

What Man?

I purposely named the title of this section "Remember the Man Caught in Adultery" to get you to ask, "What man?"

---

a   John 8:4-6
b   1 Timothy 3:16-17
c   John 8:10-11

Exactly. Where is the man who was caught in the *very act* of adultery? The Law of Moses said that both the man and the woman should be stoned,[a] yet the man was not accused.

Jesus elegantly distracted the crowd from the woman's shame, brought about justice, and showed her the path of righteousness.

> *He has shown you, O mortal, what is good.*
> *And what does the Lord require of you?*
> *To act justly and to love mercy*
> *and to walk humbly with your God. (Micah 6:8)*

Today, women pregnant out of wedlock are the obvious sinners because their growing bellies are like the Scarlet Letters of Nathaniel Hawthorne's book. Men who have extramarital sex are harder to identify. Not only that, but men who are philanderers are often looked upon as studs.

Pro-choice women recognize the unfairness.

1960s

Let's go back to the 1960s, the decade before Roe v Wade. The counterculture of the 1960s included the free love movement, which argued that sex freely entered into should not be judged by The Church or regulated by law. The result of the free love movement? Promiscuity.

What happens when couples have sex? Women get pregnant. It's simple biology.

Remember, though, that in the 1960s, women did not have equal rights to work, and single moms did not receive child support from their children's father, if they knew who the father was.

Gut check: When you read "if she knew who the father was," did you begin judging her? Remember that promiscuity applies to both women and men. The men with whom she had sex probably had multiple sex partners and may have been happy to be

---

a   Leviticus 20:10

71

anonymous. We need to acknowledge that both women and men participate in extramarital sex, so we either judge both of them or leave the judging for God.

"Do not judge so that you will not be judged." (Jesus in Matthew 7:1)

In the 1960s, my mom was in her 20s. My parents were married, and my dad was finishing his degree, so my mom's income was their main income. She worked for an upscale department store but couldn't be promoted to management because she was married and had two children at home (my sister and brother).

Mom became pregnant with me in early 1969, months before my dad finished his degree. By this time, she worked for the church and worked only through her first trimester "because that's the way it was back then."

1970S

In the 1970s, Ruth Bader Ginsburg and the ACLU went to court trying case-after-case, resulting in women's equal rights to work. Watch the 2019 movie "On the Basis of Sex, " which is a snapshot of Ruth Bader Ginsburg's life. It's a good reminder of what life was like for women in the 1970s. While watching, remember that Roe v Wade was decided January 22, 1973.

When the feminist movement changed from being pro-life to pro-choice, women thought abortion would be rare but necessary so that women were not left destitute because they couldn't work and they couldn't insist that the baby's father support them and their children. Allowing abortion seemed the fair thing to do for women.[a]

---

a   Frederica Mathewes-Green, "When Abortion Suddenly Stopped Making Sense," *National Review,* January 22, 2016, https://www.nationalreview. com/2016/01/abortion-roe-v-wade-unborn-childre n-women-feminism-march-life/.

~~The Woman Caught in Adultery~~
Jesus Saves a Woman from Injustice

Why do we call this Bible story "The Woman Caught in Adultery"? Jesus did not give it that title. The Apostle John, who wrote that gospel, did not give it that title. In truth, an editor wrote that title.

Well, I'm an editor, and I propose a new title:

"Jesus Saves a Woman from Injustice"

Let justice roll down like waters and righteousness like an ever-flowing stream. (Amos 5:24 NASB)

Suggested Prayers

Day 19

What's your worship song or hymn for today?_____

What's your posture of worship for today?

☐ dancing/giddying ☐ prostrating ☐ giving thanks
☐ praising in song/hymn ☐ kneeling ☐ confessing
☐ singing/making music ☐ serving God

John 8:1-11, Amos 5:24, Micah 6:8, Isaiah 1:17

Lord, let me remember that it takes two to get pregnant. Thank You for reminding me not to condemn the woman caught in adultery or the unseen man but instead gently bring them both back to righteousness, saying, "Go, and sin no more."

Lord, let justice roll down like waters and righteousness like an ever-flowing stream. Open my eyes to the injustices committed between the sexes, whether it is an unwillingness to pay child support, pressure to abort, coercion, abuse, rape, or sex trafficking.

Lord, show me how You want me to seek justice, help the oppressed, defend the cause of orphans, and fight for the rights of single parents.

Prayer for 40 Days for Life

Lord, thank You for protecting the 40 Days for Life worship warriors who seek justice, help the oppressed, and defend the pre-born.

DAY 20

Pray for your Country

Jesus, Author and Perfecter of faith,[a] open my mind to understand the Scriptures.[b]

Taken

Daniel 1:1-20, 6:1-28, 9:4-19

Screams and yells pierced the air as foreign soldiers drove advisors, legislators, and royalty of every age to the leader of the raid, King Nebuchadnezzar. He commanded and the soldiers obeyed. The soldiers herded the captives north and then followed the Euphrates river down to Babylon. It was a long walk, perhaps two months' time.

The Babylonian roads were littered with people. The palace was a marvel to see. A beautiful garden seemed to hang on the tier.[c] Oh, but to rest in that splendor!

---

a   Hebrews 12:2
b   Luke 24:45
c   The Hanging Gardens of Babylon were among the Seven Wonders of the Ancient World.

The captives were given water while the king barked orders. His words were unfamiliar, but it was clear that he ordered Ashpenaz to choose from among the men. He was to choose royalty, good-looking young men who showed knowledge, understanding, and wisdom. Among those chosen were Hananiah, Mishael, Azariah, and Daniel.

Before the raid, the young men had their whole lives ahead of them. They had studied the Scriptures, their history, and how to govern. They were destined to advise the King of Judah and administer under his leadership. Until the raid, that was King Jehoiakim.

The chosen young men quickly learned the language and literature of their captors. King Nebuchadnezzar sent food and wine from his own table and commanded that after three years, they would serve him.

Eating the king's food and adding to their scholarly endeavors was better than the exile for most of their fellow Judeans, but they missed their families, the holy city of Jerusalem, and the beauty of Solomon's temple.

They were given new names, names that honored the foreign god Bel (Baal). No longer Hananiah, Mishael, and Azariah but instead Shadrach, Meshach, and Abednigo. Daniel was renamed Belteshazzar—from "God is my judge" to "Bel's treasurer."

They had every reason to be bitter.

The Daniel Diet

Daniel knew that the king's food was unclean according to the Law of Moses, and he did not want to dishonor God. He could have indulged to console himself, but instead he approached Ashpenaz, asking permission to eat food that allowed him to keep his promise to God.

"Daniel, you are my favorite, but do not ask this of me. I cannot lose favor with the king. Why should he see you weaker than others your age? It is my life that I may lose."

"Please test my friends and me for ten days," Daniel replied. "Give us nothing but vegetables to eat and water to drink. Then compare us with the young men who eat the king's food. See how we look. After that, treat us according to what you see."

The chief official agreed. After 10 days, he was surprised. Hananiah, Mishael, Azariah, and Daniel looked healthier than the men who ate the royal food. So, from that time on, they ate vegetables and water to honor God.

At the end of the three years, Ashpenaz presented all the young men to King Nebuchadnezzar, but the king was most impressed by Hananiah, Mishael, Azariah, and Daniel, so he chose them to serve him.

Daniel served the king while remaining righteous in the sight of the Lord. He interpreted King Nebuchadnezzar's dreams and served him well.

After the king died, King Belshazzar ruled for a short time before the Persians conquered the Babylonians.

Daniel's Righteousness

By this time, Daniel was over 80 years old. King Darius, the Persian, ruled and quickly observed the wisdom of Daniel, making him one of the three top administrators. Because of his extraordinary spirit, Daniel became even more distinguished, so King Darius planned to put him above all, only second to the king himself.

The administrators and those who reported to them were jealous and began looking for evidence that Daniel was corrupt but to no avail.

They devised a new plan and approached King Darius, saying:

"King Darius, live forever! All your advisors and leaders have consulted together that the king should establish a statute that anyone who makes a petition to any god or man besides you for thirty days, shall be cast into the lions' den.

"Now, O king, establish the injunction and sign the document so that it may not be changed, according to the law, which may not be revoked."

a   Daniel 6:6-8 NASB with a few repetitive words removed

Their appeal to the king's pride succeeded, and King Darius signed the injunction.

Daniel, knowing the document was signed, entered the roof chamber of his house and knelt before the west windows, which were open toward Jerusalem, three times a day, praying and giving thanks before God just as he had done before. He was easily caught.

The administrators and those who reported to them approached the king again.

> *"Did you not sign an injunction that any man who makes a petition to any god or man besides you, O king, for thirty days, is to be cast into the lions' den?"*

> *The king replied, "The statement is true, according to the law, which may not be revoked."*

> *They answered, "Daniel, who is one of the exiles from Judah, pays no attention to you, O king, or to the injunction which you signed, but keeps making his petition three times a day."*

> *As soon as the king heard this statement, he was deeply distressed and set his mind on delivering Daniel.*

> *Then these men came to the king and said, "Recognize, O king, that it is a law that no injunction may be changed."*

> *The king gave orders, and (80+ year old) Daniel was brought in and cast into the lions' den. The king spoke and said to Daniel, "Your God whom you constantly serve will Himself deliver you."*

> *A stone was brought and laid over the mouth of the den; and the king sealed it with his own signet ring and with the signet rings of his nobles, so that nothing would be changed in regard to Daniel.*

The king went off to his palace and spent the night fasting. No entertainment was brought before him; and his sleep fled from him.

The king arose at the break of day and went in haste to the lions' den. He cried out with a troubled voice. "Daniel, servant of the living God, has your God been able to deliver you from the lions?"

Daniel spoke, "O king, live forever! My God sent His angel and shut the lions' mouths, and they have not harmed me, inasmuch as I was found innocent before Him; and also toward you, O king, I have committed no crime."

Daniel was found innocent.

The king was very pleased and gave orders for Daniel to be taken up out of the den. No injury whatever was found on him because he had trusted in his God.

The king then gave orders, and they brought those men who had maliciously accused Daniel, and they cast them, their children and their wives into the lions' den; and they had not reached the bottom of the den before the lions overpowered them and crushed all their bones.

Then Darius the king wrote to all the peoples, nations, and men of every language who were living in all the land:

> *"May your peace abound! I make a decree that in all the dominion of my kingdom men are to fear and tremble before the God of Daniel.*
>
> *"For He is the living God and enduring forever, And His kingdom is one which will not be destroyed, And His dominion will be forever. He delivers and rescues and performs signs and wonders in heaven and on earth, Who has also delivered* **Daniel from the power of the lions."**

So, this Daniel enjoyed success in the reign of Darius and in the reign of Cyrus the Persian.[a]

At about this same time, Daniel observed that according to Jeremiah's prophecy, the end of the exile was soon approaching, so he prayed for his people.

In his prayer, Daniel confessed to God saying, "We have sinned"[b] and "We have not listened."[c] Even though he was found innocent in God's eyes and therefore protected in the lions' den, Daniel identified with his people and said, "*We* have sinned" instead of "*They* have sinned."

Daniel was over 80 years old when he was put in the lions' den, yet the Lord sent an angel to shut the lions' mouths because Daniel was found innocent in God's eyes.[d] Eighty years to sin and confess, sin and confess, and he had nothing left to confess, no one left to forgive—he was innocent because he confessed and forgave continuously while keeping his eyes on God and honoring Him.

Identifying with the People

Yet around the same time, Daniel fasted in sackcloth and ashes and prayed: "*We* have sinned, committed iniquity, acted wickedly,

---

a   Daniel 6:12-28 NASB with a few repetitive words removed
b   Daniel 9:5
c   Daniel 9:6
d   Daniel 6:22

rebelled, turned aside from Your ordinances, and have not listened to Your prophets"[a] and "Open shame belongs to *us*."[b]

Daniel was clearly a righteous man, so innocent that not one scratch from a lion was found on him,[c] yet he did not pray saying "the people have sinned" nor "open shame belong to them."

Instead, he identified himself with his people as he confessed their sins and petitioned the Lord to rebuild the city of Jerusalem, not for any merits of his or the people's but because of God's great compassion.[d]

—∞—

"Why doesn't God end abortion?" my husband asked in an exasperated voice.

"Because Christians don't want it!" I heard myself say, "If they did, they wouldn't have abortions or extramarital sex!"

Those words were not my own. They flew out of me, and then I heard them.

Of all abortions in the U.S., 36% are by women who go to church at least once per month.[e] Our most recent abortion statistics are from 2017, so let's apply the 36% to the 862,320 abortions in that year: >310,000.

---

a   Daniel 9:5-6
b   Daniel 9:8
c   Daniel 6:23
d   Daniel 9:18
e   Care-Net, "Study of Women Who Have Had an Abortion & Their Views on Church." (PDF, 2016) Go to https://resources.care-net.org/ free-resources/ to get a copy.
Additional statistics can be found at:
Jenna Jerman, Rachel K. Jones, and Tsuyoshi Onda, "Characteristics of U.S. Abortion Patients in 2014 and Changes Since 2008," Guttmacher Institute, May 2016, https://www.guttmacher.org/report/ characteristics-us-abortion-patients-2014#full-article
The Institute for Pro-Life Advancement, "Views of Pastors on abortion and involvement of Churches in the Pro-Life Movement," https://media.wix.com/ ugd/59e9ba_fa5766a950e24408acb660284b0dd666.pdf

Why is that number not zero?

One third of those are by women who go to church at least once per week: >102,000.

Why is that number not zero?

Note that we have no statistics on the men who got them pregnant.

Of all women who have abortions, 70% indicate their religious preference is Christian. Not my denomination, you say?

Among all abortions, women listed their religious preferences as shown in the chart.

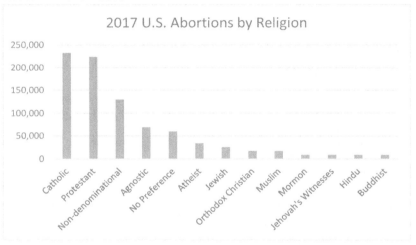

Let us not be quick to judge non-Christians for choosing abortion when Christians are aborting. Let us not be quick to judge other denominations for Jesus did command us to be divided but to be one in Him.

> *"I do not pray for these alone, but also for those who will believe in Me through their word; that they all may be one, as You, Father, are in Me, and I in You; that they also may be one in Us, that the world may believe that You sent Me.*

"And the glory which You gave Me I have given them, that they may be one just as We are one: I in them, and You in Me; that they may be made perfect in one, and that the world may know that You have sent Me, and have loved them as You have loved Me." (John 17:20-23 NKJV)

Now I plead with you, brethren, by the name of our Lord Jesus Christ, that you all speak the same thing, and that there be no divisions among you, but that you be perfectly joined together in the same mind and in the same judgment. Now I say this, that each of you says, "I am of Paul," or "I am of Apollos," or "I am of Cephas," or "I am of Christ." Is Christ divided? Was Paul crucified for you? Or were you baptized in the name of Paul? (1 Corinthians 1:10, 12-13 NKJV)

—⁓—

Let us be like Daniel: innocent yet identifying with our people who have sinned. Daniel identified with the people of Judah. Let's identify with the people of The Church and our country.

Daniel was found innocent,[a] so we can also be found innocent. Repeat the prayers in Days 6-17 if needed so that you, too, can be found innocent.

It's the ultimate act of agape love to come before the King of kings in humbleness on behalf of other people.

---
a   Daniel 6:21

Suggested Prayers

Today's suggested prayer is Daniel 9:4-19 adapted to today's abortion pandemic.

Day 20

What's your worship song or hymn for today?_____

What's your posture of worship for today?

☐ dancing/giddying   ☐ prostrating   ☐ giving thanks
☐ praising in song/hymn   ☐ kneeling   ☐ confessing
☐ singing/making music   ☐ serving God

Daniel 9:4-19, 1 Corinthians 10:15

Lord, You are my great and awesome God. You keep Your covenant of love with those who love You and choose Your ways.

Lord, we have sinned and done wrong. We have been wicked and have rebelled. We have turned away from Your ways. We have not listened to You or those who speak in Your name.

Lord, You are righteous, but this day we are covered with shame—the people of our country and Christians both near and far in all the countries where you have scattered us. We, our political leaders, and our ancestors are covered with shame, Lord, because we have sinned against You through extramarital sex, unfair treatment of those caught in adultery, and abortion.

Lord our God, You are merciful and forgiving, even though we have rebelled against You. We have not obeyed You or kept Your ways of purity before, during, and after marriage between one man and one woman "until death do us part." We have turned away, refusing to choose You.

Therefore, the consequences have poured out on us because we have sinned against You. Consequences have come on us, yet we have not sought the favor of the Lord our God by turning from our sins and giving attention to Your truth. You are righteous in everything You do, yet we have not obeyed You.

Lord our God, who broke us free with a mighty hand and who made for Yourself a name that endures to this day, we have sinned. We have done wrong.

Lord, in keeping with all your righteous acts, turn away Your anger and Your wrath from us. Our sins and the iniquities of our ancestors have made Christians an object of scorn to all those around us.

Now, our God, hear the prayers and petitions of Your servants. For your sake, Lord, look with favor on your desolate people. Give ear, our God, and hear; open Your eyes and see the desolation of our country. We do not make requests of You because we are righteous, but because of Your great mercy.

Lord, listen!

Lord, forgive!

Lord, hear and act!

For Your sake, my God, do not delay, because your people bear Your Name.

Prayer for 40 Days for Life

Lord, thank You for keeping Your covenant of love with the worship warriors at abortion facilities around the world. Thank You for being merciful and forgiving to those women and men at the abortion facilities. Hear the prayers and petitions of my sisters and brothers who are praying and counseling at abortion facilities. Look with favor on those seeking abortions and providing abortions. Forgive them. Open their eyes to Your love. Show them the way out of temptation. Thank You for your great mercy. Thank You for Your forgiveness.

DAY 21

Consider the Woman at the Well

J esus, thirst quencher,[a] open my mind to understand the Scriptures.[b]

Thirsty

John 4:1-45

After the Passover celebration in Jerusalem,[c] Jesus and His followers walked north along the Jordan River on their way to Galilee. They stopped where Jesus had been baptized, and then His disciples baptized others in the Jordan River.[d]

When the Pharisees heard that Jesus was baptizing more people than John, Jesus and His disciples left for Galilee. Traveling north along the river would have been their usual route, but Jesus "had to go to Samaria,"[e] which was northwest up into the mountains.

---

a   John 4:14
b   Luke 24:45
c   John 2:23
d   John 3:22-23
e   John 4:1-4

Samaria was not on the route most people took from Jerusalem to Galilee. Walking along the Jordan River would have been much easier than climbing uphill to Samaria.

Someone today might say, "I felt led to go to Samaria" or "God led me to Samaria" or "The Spirit led me to Samaria." These are all ways to express having a felt need to go. John, the writer of the gospel, was saying that Jesus had a "felt need" to go to Samaria.

Tired and hungry, Jesus and His disciples stopped near Sychar at Jacob's well to rest.[a] His disciples went into the city to buy food while Jesus stayed behind.[b] While the disciples were gone, a Samaritan woman came to the well by herself.[c]

Usually, women go to the well together because they like to socialize while they work. Some biblical scholars[d] say that the woman came at 6 a.m. on the Roman time system because the Apostle John was writing his gospel after the Temple was destroyed, saying that most women usually went to the well at night not the morning, which matches up with Genesis 24:11, which says that toward evening, women go to draw water.

Other biblical scholars say that "the 6th hour" was the Hebrew time system, meaning that the Samaritan woman was there around 12 noon, in the heat of the day, when most women would avoid the well. Instead, women would be there first thing in the morning to get the water they needed for the day.

No matter which scholar you believe, clearly the woman was there by herself, presumably because she was ostracized by other women for having had five husbands and living out of wedlock with her current beau.

The Samaritan woman approached the well but avoided looking at Jesus. Clearly, he was a Jew. She knew that Jews looked down upon Samaritans, and she had no respect for Jews, either.

Jesus said to her, "Please give me a drink of water."

a John 4:5-6
b John 4:8
c John 4:6, 7
d Dr. Bill Creasy, "John," Logos Bible Study, 2011. Audible, 11 hr., 42 min.

Indignant, maybe even curtly, she said, "Why would you, a Jewish man, ask me, a Samaritan woman, for a drink of water?"

Jesus answered, "If only you knew who I am and the gift God wants to give to you, you'd ask Me for a drink, and I would give you living water."

"Living water? But sir, you don't even have a bucket!" she said indignantly. "Do you really think that you are greater than our ancestor Jacob, who gave us this well and drank of it himself along with his sons and livestock?"

Kindly, Jesus replied, "Everyone who drinks of this water will thirst again, but anyone who drinks the living water that comes from Me will be forever satisfied. My living water becomes a well inside her body, springing up life!"

Jesus often taught using analogies and metaphors. Perhaps He taught this way because He was looking for people who would seek to understand His deeper meaning.

> *"Anyone who drinks the living water that comes from Me will be forever satisfied."*

In this exchange, Jesus was checking to see if the Samaritan woman was willing to seek understanding. Perhaps she didn't want to listen and instead responded in a snide way, saying, "Give me this water you talk of so that I don't have to come back here by myself day after day."

Jesus, knowing her real heartache, said, "Go get your husband, and bring him back here."

Indignant that she must have a man to make her worthy of this living water, she said, "I have no husband."

"That's true," Jesus said kindly. "You have had five husbands, but now you're living with a man who is not your husband. You tell the truth."

She looked surprised. Caught off guard, she wondered how He could know how many men she had. She said, "You must be a prophet."

She didn't want to talk about her infidelities, so she changed the subject, trying to pick a fight to distract Him from her sins. She pointed up and said, "Our fathers taught us to worship on this mountain, but you Jews say that Jerusalem is the place for worship." Jesus did not correct her, but He recognized that she did not know all of her people's history.

A Little Samaritan History

Israel Split into Two Kingdoms

The people of Israel (also called the Jews or the Hebrews) were not always one country. The people of Israel had been led by Moses out of Egypt and then by Joshua into the Promised Land. They lived in the land with no king until King Saul, who was followed by Kings David and Solomon.

Solomon's son King Rehoboam was not as wise as his father and made the northern tribes angry by not relieving them from unfair pay for hard labor.[a] In 1 King 12:19, we learn that the nine northern tribes split from Judah and Benjamin in the south and made Jeroboam their king.

From the time of Joshua until the beginning of Rehoboam's reign, the Jews were of the same heritage and also one country, called Israel both by heritage and by lines on a map.

After the northern tribes split off, the northern people, although sharing the same heritage, now had different lines on a map and called themselves Israel. The southern kingdom was called Judah (and later Judea).

Jeroboam of the northern kingdom of Israel knew that The Law of Moses said the Israelites were to travel to the temple in Jerusalem

---

a   1 Kings 12:4

three times per year for Passover (in the spring), Pentecost (50 days after Passover), and Tabernacles (in the fall), providing three opportunities each year for the hearts of "his" people to return to the king of Judah.

Idol Worship on This Mountain

Jeroboam couldn't risk losing his people to the southern kingdom, so he made two golden calves, which were idols of Egypt. He set one at Dan in the north and one at Bethel near the border of Judah—Bethel was "on this mountain" where the Samaritan woman's ancestors worshiped.[a]

Exiled and Intermarried

The Samaritans, however, were not just the descendants of the northern kingdom of Israel. Their heritage included intermarriages with the Assyrians, who brutally took them from Israel and kept them captive for about 180 years.

The Kingdom of Judah was later taken away by the Babylonians but were able to return to Jerusalem after 70 years to rebuild. The Samaritans were of mixed heritage, whereas, the Jews were "purebred" descendants of Jacob's sons Judah, Benjamin, and Levi.

As the Samaritan woman said, the Samaritans had worshiped in Dan and Bethel, but of course many centuries before that, Moses gave The Law that explained the requirements of Passover, Pentecost, and The Tabernacles to all the descendants of Jacob.

Location Location Location

Jesus, of course, knew the Samaritan and the Jewish histories. He pointed out that the Samaritan woman's people didn't know who they were worshiping but the Jews did.[b]

---

a   1 Kings 12:26-33
b   John 4:22

More importantly, Jesus directed her attention to the new thing God was doing.[a] No longer would Bethel or Jerusalem serve as "the" place to worship. Instead, true worshipers would "worship in spirit and truth."[b] But what does that mean?

What Does It Mean to Worship in Spirit and Truth?

About 40 years after Jesus ascended to heaven, the Romans destroyed the Temple in 70 AD during the Siege of Jerusalem, and it has not been rebuilt. Since 70 AD, it has not been possible to worship God in the temple for Passover, Pentecost, and Tabernacles as Moses' Law says to do.

We also know, from the Apostle Paul's letters, that a person has a spirit, a soul, and a body[c] and that the body is the temple of the Holy Spirit.[d] So, when Jesus foretold that true worshipers would worship in spirit, He meant that they would worship from inside their bodies no matter where in the world their bodies were.

True worshipers worship from inside their bodies.

Now a location on a map is no longer important. Going to a building is no longer required to find God. Now, true worshipers worship in their spirits and in the truth of who God is and what He has done for us.

Finding Satisfaction in All the Wrong Places

However, Jesus was saying even more than that.

The Samaritan woman knew the truth about marriage. She knew that she should have been married only once. That's the truth of how God designed the world. That was why she was shamed

---

a   Isaiah 43:19; Although God is the same yesterday, today, and forever (Hebrews 13:8), He does not do the same things throughout history.

b   John 4:23-24

c   1 Thessalonians 5:23, see also Luke 1:46, Hebrews 4:12

d   1 Corinthians 3:16, 6:19

by other women and why she felt ashamed enough to go to the well by herself.

She wanted satisfaction from her relationships, but when she didn't feel satisfied by "that old water," she went looking for "new water." When that "water" didn't satisfy, she went looking for "new water" again and repeatedly until she had been with at least six men. Jesus was offering her satisfying "water"—living water, which only He can give.

How many people do you know who look for satisfaction from "well water" rather than "living water"?

Like the Samaritan woman, we are offered the satisfaction of living water:

- It doesn't matter that we are not Jews. Jesus came for the whole world.[a]

- It doesn't matter that we have been shamed or feel ashamed for not following God's laws. Jesus did not come into the world to condemn the world.[b]

- It doesn't matter that we have been following the religious rituals of our ancestors. Jesus came to give us rest.[c]

The Samaritan woman was so enamored with this living water, with the kindness of Jesus, and with the knowledge that He is the Messiah that she ran back to town and told everyone about Him.[d] Many people came to faith in Jesus because of her.[e]

---

a   John 3:16
b   John 3:17
c   Matthew 11:28
d   John 4:28-30
e   John 4:39-42

History of Abortion in the U.S.

Also like the Samaritan woman, most of us do not know our history. Go to MybodyMyworship.com/history-of-abortion. html to learn about the history of abortion in the U.S. or you can ascertain the history from the suggested prayer.

If you do not live in the U.S., please incorporate your own country's abortion history into your prayers.

Suggested Prayers

Day 21

What's your worship song or hymn for today?_____

What's your posture of worship for today?

☐ dancing/giddying ☐ prostrating ☐ giving thanks
☐ praising in song/hymn ☐ kneeling ☐ confessing
☐ singing/making music ☐ serving God

John 4:7-45; Philippians 2:3; James 1:5, 4:7; 1 John 4:8; Exodus 20:5-6; Ezekiel 18: 1-4, 20; Matthew 18:6; Romans 5:18, Ephesians 6:13-14

Lord, the woman at the well got Samaritan history partially right, but she did not know all that You wrote in The Law[a] and in the history books.[b] Let us be different. Let *us* not be ignorant of Your ways or our own history of both illegal and legal abortion.

Lord, we and our ancestors have allowed sin, and we're sorry. We allowed Margaret Sanger's advancement of birth control then hormonal birth control, which aborts babies before we even know we have conceived. For this, we apologize, Lord.

We allowed Sanger to target minorities and today in New York City more Black babies are aborted than born alive.[c] For this, we apologize, Lord.

We point at Sanger's racist history, but we neglect to search our own hearts for times when we have not regarded others more than ourselves.[d] For this, we apologize, Lord.

---

a The first five books of the Bible
b Particularly 1 Kings and 2 Chronicles
c Jason L. Riley, "Let's Talk About the Black Abortion Rate," *The Wall Street Journal*, July 10, 2018, https://www.wsj.com/articles/lets-talk-about-the-black-abortion-rate-1531263697.
d Philippians 2:3

We complain about the high abortion rates among Black and Hispanic Americans,[a] but we do not take responsibility for the governmental programs that keep people in poverty or encourage single motherhood. For this, we apologize, Lord.

We believed Alfred Kinsey's research, *Sexual Behavior in the Human Male* and *Sexual Behavior in the Human Female*, which showed that homosexuality was much more prevalent than it actually was. For this, we apologize, Lord.

We paid for *Playboy* and other pornography, which exploits women. For this, we apologize, Lord.

We paid and are still paying women less for the same work, and it took us too long to create fair employment policies. For this, we apologize, Lord.

We did not support women and their children who were abandoned by their husbands, and even today we struggle to have equitable and safe resolutions in our divorce decrees. For this, we apologize, Lord.

We allowed the free sex movement, resulting in single motherhood and the desperation for safe, legal abortion. For this, we apologize, Lord.

In the 1960s, when NARAL said large numbers of women were dying from back-alley abortions, we believed them rather than checking the facts. For this, we apologize, Lord.

When NARAL campaigned against the Catholic church's pro-life stance, The Church stood by rather than standing firm with our Christian sisters and brothers. For this, we apologize, Lord.

When Roe won her case against Wade and Doe won her case against Bolton, we did not succeed in creating a constitutional

---

[a]   In the U.S., five times more Black babies are aborted than white and three times more Hispanic babies are aborted than white according to:
Susan A. Cohen, "Abortion and Women of Color: The Bigger Picture," August 6, 2008, *Guttmacher Policy Review* 11, no. 3, https://www.guttmacher.org/gpr/2008/08/abortion-and-women-color-bigger-picture#

amendment to protect the rights of the pre-born. For this, we apologize, Lord.

We allowed Your name to be removed from public school and for sex education to be full of partial truths and void of scientific support. For this, we apologize, Lord.

We have allowed modern medicine to promote abortion, aborti-facients, hormonal "treatment" for those who call themselves transgender, and sex reassignment surgeries, all of which take away our reproduction. For this, we apologize, Lord.

Forgive us, Lord, for allowing the lies of the enemy in the name of "love" to win over the truth of Your agape love.

We have allowed children to be molested by our church leaders in multiple denominations. We have allowed women to be sex-ually harassed in the workplace and in our churches. For this, we apologize, Lord.

Lord, forgive The Church for not following You and Your ways. Increase our knowledge and understanding. Give us wisdom. From this day forward, we choose to stand firm in the truth.

Show us how to follow Your examples of sharing the truth through love to all non-believers so that they would see You for who You are—for You are agape love. Use new believers to bring all in their own communities to belief in Your love like the woman at the well brought her community to Christ and encourage us to mentor new believers so that they become disciples.

Prayer for 40 Days for Life

Lord, thank You for protecting the sidewalk counselors as they stand firm with the belt of truth, which holds all their armor in place.

Battle

DAY 22

Pray for Post-Abortive Women & Men

J esus, restorer,[a] open my mind to understand the scriptures.[b]

Control

2 Samuel 11:1-12:25, Psalm 51, Psalm 32

King David, the great warrior who leads his Mighty Men to take more of the land God promised his people, stayed home from battle. Perhaps he was bored with his success.

The king couldn't sleep. He got up from his bed and went up to his rooftop for some air. He looked out upon the land the Lord had given His people. His Mighty Men had built homes near his own in Jerusalem. He could see the Tent of Meeting nearby as well.

A soft light caught the king's eye. He peered and saw a stunning woman bathing. He was mesmerized by her beauty.

---

a   1 Peter 5:10
b   Luke 24:45

David called to his servants, "Who is the woman who lives there?"

One answered, "Is this not Bathsheba, the daughter of Eliam, the wife of Uriah the Hittite?"[a]

Her husband and father are away at battle, thought the king. He said, "Send messengers. Bring her to me."

When the woman entered his presence, she said, "My king, how may I serve you?"

David gazed at her beauty. "Your husband is away?"

David's servants knew of his adultery.

"Yes, my king. He is in battle at Rabbah."

"Perhaps while he is away, you would accompany me."

Embarrassed by his interest, she said, "What if we are found out?"

"He is away," David said. "How will he know?"

How can I say, "No" to the king? she thought. *What if my husband loses favor because of my refusal?*

David gently took her to his bed and lay with her. Afterwards, she purified herself from her uncleanness[b] and returned to her house.

Several weeks later, she reasoned that she had conceived and went to see King David.

"I am pregnant," she said.

"No! Oh, no!" the king said, pacing. "Do not worry. I know what to do."

As she left his palace, he called his messenger. "Ride to Joab immediately and say to him, 'Send me Uriah the Hittite.'"

Uriah returned to Jerusalem and reported to the king, who asked, "How are Joab and the men?"

"He is well, my lord," Uriah responded. "The men fight valiantly."

---

a   Eliam and Uriah were among David's Mighty Men (2 Samuel 23:34, 39;
    1 Chronicles 11:31). David's counselor, Ahithophel, was the father of Eliam
    (2 Samuel 23:34; 15:12, 31).
b   Leviticus 15:18

David continued, "Tell me the state of the war." Uriah reported on the battles and victories. "Good to hear. Good to hear," David said. "Thank you for the good report. Now go down to your house and wash your feet." Uriah went out of the king's house.

King David sent his servant out with a present for Uriah and his wife, but Uriah did not go down to his house. Instead, Uriah slept at the door of the king's house with all the servants of his lord.

The next morning, the servants told the king that Uriah did not go down to his house. David summoned him. When Uriah entered the king's presence, David said, "Have you not come from a journey? Why did you not go down to your house?"

Uriah said to David, "The ark and Israel and Judah are staying in temporary shelters, and my lord Joab and the servants of my lord are camping in the open field. Shall I then go to my house to eat and to drink and to lie with my wife? By your life and the life of your soul, I will not do this thing."

David replied, "Stay here today also, and tomorrow I will let you go."

David invited Uriah to dinner, and he ate and drank. David made him drunk. In the evening, Uriah went out to lie on his bed with his lord's servants.

David's servants knew his plan to deceive Uriah.

Again, the servants said, "Uriah did not go down to his house."

David, worried, considered a new plan. He wrote a letter to Joab, saying, "Place Uriah in the front line of the fiercest battle and withdraw from him, so that he may be struck down and die." He secured the letter with his royal seal and sent it with Uriah as he returned to Rabbah.

Joab considered his orders. *If only Uriah dies,* he reasoned, *all the men will know he died by the hand of the king. These men must remain loyal to the king.*

Joab put Uriah among valiant men and sent them near the city. Ammonites came out from the city to fight while others shot arrows from the city wall. Some of David's men fell, including Uriah.

Joab sent a messenger to Jerusalem to report the events of the war. When the messenger entered the king's presence, he said, "The men prevailed against us and came out against us in the field, but we pressed them as far as the entrance of the gate. Moreover, the archers shot at your servants from the wall, so some of the king's servants are dead, and your servant Uriah the Hittite is also dead."

When the wife of Uriah heard that Uriah her husband was dead, she mourned for her husband.

When the time of mourning was over, David brought her to his house, and she became his wife. She bore him a son.

What David had done was evil in the sight of the Lord, so He sent the prophet Nathan to speak to the king.

> David suppressed his sin and went on living his life the way he wanted.

When he entered the king's presence, Nathan said, "There were two men in one city, the one rich and the other poor.

"The rich man had a great many flocks and herds.

"But the poor man had nothing except one little ewe lamb, which he bought and nourished. The lamb was like a daughter to him.

"Now a traveler came to the rich man, and the rich man was unwilling to take from his own flock or his own herd to prepare for the wayfarer. Instead, he took the poor man's ewe lamb and prepared it for the man who had come to him."

David's anger burned greatly against the man, and he said to Nathan, "As the Lord lives, surely the man who has done this deserves to die. He must make restitution for the lamb fourfold, because he did this thing and had no compassion."

Nathan then said to David, "You are the man! Thus says the Lord God of Israel,

> 'It is I who anointed you king over Israel, and it is I who delivered you from the hand of Saul. I also gave you your

master's house and your master's wives into your care, and I gave you the house of Israel and Judah. If that had been too little, I would have added to you many more things like these!

'Why have you despised the word of the Lord[a] by doing evil in His sight? You have struck down Uriah the Hittite with the sword and have taken his wife to be your wife.

'Now therefore, the sword shall never depart from your house, because you have despised Me.

'Behold, I will raise up evil against you from your own household. I will even take your wives before your eyes and give them to your companion, and he will lie with your wives in broad daylight. Indeed you did it secretly, but I will do this thing before all Israel.'[b]

Then David cried and said to Nathan, "I have sinned against the Lord!"

Nathan said, "The Lord also has taken away your sin; you shall not die. However, because by this deed you have given occasion to the enemies of the Lord to blaspheme, the child also that is born to you shall surely die." Nathan left.

David, sobbing, ran to the Tent of Meeting and cried out to the Lord, singing:

"Be gracious to me, O God, according to Your lovingkindness. According to the greatness of Your compassion blot out my transgressions. Wash me thoroughly from my iniquity and cleanse me from my sin. For I know my transgressions, and my sin is ever before me. Against You, You only, I have sinned and done what is evil in Your sight, so You are justified when You speak and blameless when You judge.

---

a   The king is responsible for knowing the law according to Deuteronomy 17:18-20, and of course adultery is against the law (Exodus 20:14, Deuteronomy 5:18) as is murder (Exodus 20:13; Deuteronomy 5:17)—both of which had legal consequences of capital punishment (Leviticus 20:10; 24:17).

b   2 Samuel 12:7-12 NASB with a few redundant words removed

"Behold, You desire truth in the innermost being, and in the hidden part You will make me know wisdom. Purify me with hyssop, and I shall be clean. Wash me, and I shall be whiter than snow. Make me to hear joy and gladness. Let the bones that You have broken rejoice. Hide Your face from my sins and blot out all my iniquities.

"Create in me a clean heart, O God, and renew a steadfast spirit within me. Do not cast me away from Your presence and do not take Your Holy Spirit from me. Restore to me the joy of Your salvation and sustain me with a willing spirit. Then I will teach transgressors Your ways, and sinners will be converted to You."[a]

Then the baby boy Uriah's widow bore to David became very sick. David inquired of God for the child. He fasted and went and lay all night on the ground. On the seventh day, the child died.

David saw that his servants were whispering together. He asked, "Is the child dead?"

They said, "He is dead."

David arose from the ground, washed, anointed himself, and changed his clothes. He came into the Tent of Meeting and worshiped. When he returned to his palace, his servants set food before him and he ate.

David comforted his wife Bathsheba,[b] and lay with her. She conceived again and gave birth to a son, whom he named him Solomon.

---

a   Psalm 51:1-13, but go read the whole chapter!

b   Bathsheba is referenced by name in 2 Samuel 11:3 but not again until 12:24. In between, she is referred to as Uriah's wife, leaving the emphasis on David. Some Jewish and Christian scholars assert that David raped Bathsheba. I do not go that far because the Hebrew word for *force* used in the story of Shechem raping Dinah (see Genesis 34:2) and in the story of Amnon raping Tamar (see 2 Samuel 13:12-14) are not used in the story of David and Bathsheba. Yet the emphasis on David's actions, the social status of women and wives at the time, David's position as king, Bathsheba's grandfather Ahithophel conspiring against David (2 Samuel 15:12, 31), and David recompensing Bathsheba by making her Queen Mother all indicate that Bathsheba was not pursuing adultery.

David returned to the Tent of Meeting and worshiped the Lord in song:

"How blessed is he whose transgression is forgiven, whose sin is covered! How blessed is the man to whom the Lord does not impute iniquity, and in whose spirit there is no deceit!

"When I kept silent about my sin, my body wasted away through my groaning all day long. For day and night Your hand was heavy upon me. My vitality was drained away as with the fever heat of summer.

"I acknowledged my sin to You, and my iniquity I did not hide. I said, 'I will confess my transgressions to the Lord,' and You forgave the guilt of my sin.

"Therefore, let everyone who is godly pray to You in a time when You may be found that they may not drown in the floodwaters of judgment. You are my hiding place. You preserve me from trouble. You surround me with songs of deliverance.

The king heard God's response:

'I will instruct you and teach you in the way which you should go. I will counsel you with My eye upon you.

'Many are the sorrows of the wicked, but he who trusts in the Lord, lovingkindness shall surround him. Be glad in the Lord and rejoice, you righteous ones, and shout for joy, all you who are upright in heart.'"[a]

---

a   Psalm 32:1-8, 10-11 NASB with a few words in verse 6 from NLT

The Spiritual Effects of Abortion

After I was healed from my abortion, I asked God what had happened to me spiritually. I knew I felt different from the time of my abortion until I reconciled with God. I remember saying that I was like the walking dead—and I said that before there was a TV show by that name. I was going about life, but I was dead inside until I chose Christ and confessed my sins.

Lord, I prayed, *there are no stories of abortion in the Bible. Is there a story that explains what happened to me?*

God led me to the story of David and Bathsheba. I had studied David's life twice before, but I studied it again. I mentioned to my pastor that God had led me to this story. He said that this story is about David's need to control. That resonated with me. When I had my crisis pregnancy, I needed to control.

King David's story is about controling his circumstances. The same is true for abortion..

Like David, I had extramarital sex resulting in a crisis pregnancy.

Like David, I wanted to cover up my sin. He arranged for Uriah to die; I arranged for my baby to die.

Like David, I moved on with life and didn't think about what I had done. Nathan brought David's sin to his attention. Jesus brought my sin to my attention, but He was much more gentle than Nathan!

David immediately realized his sin. I, however, blamed everyone else. God kindly said to me,

> *"Come now, and let us reason together. Though your sins are as scarlet, they will be as white as snow." (Isaiah 1:18 NASB)*

When I accepted responsibility, He washed me clean[a] and renewed a steadfast spirit within me.[b]

---

a   Psalm 51:2, 7
b   Psalm 51:10

When I told my story to 200 people at a church gathering, I said that I was washed whiter than snow. I didn't know where those words came from! Later when I studied David's story, I found "white as snow" in his Psalm 51:7 and in Isaiah 1:18. (You can read more of my "coming to Jesus" story in chapter 4 of *ReTested*.)

The Walking Dead

In Psalm 32, David elegantly described what happened while he had unconfessed sin of extramarital sex and murder:

When I kept silent about my sin, my body wasted away through my groaning all day long. For day and night Your hand was heavy upon me; my vitality was drained away as with the fever heat of summer. I acknowledged my sin to You and my iniquity I did not hide. I said, "I will confess my transgressions to the Lord"; and You forgave the guilt of my sin. (Psalm 32:3-5 NASB, emphasis mine)

That was it! My vitality was drained away until I acknowledged my sin! That's why I felt like the walking dead—I had no vitality.

From David's Psalms 32 and 51, we learn what happens when we murder and commit adultery:

- When we keep silent about our sin, our bodies waste away.[a]
- The Lord's hand is heavy upon us.[b]
- Our vitality is drained away.[c]
- We yearn to hear joy and gladness again.[d]
- We can't wait for our broken bones to rejoice.[e]
- We want to be renewed with a steadfast spirit.[f]

---

a   Psalm 32:3
b   Psalm 32:4
c   Psalm 32:4
d   Psalm 51:8
e   Psalm 51:8
f   Psalm 51:10

- We want to feel the Holy Spirit within us.[a]
- We want to be restored with the joy of salvation.[b]

For some women and men, the above list from Psalms 32 and 51 describes depression. I, however, was never diagnosed with depression and never exhibited today's signs of depression. Until Jesus showed me what I had done, I felt justified and had no regrets. Now that I have the joy of the Lord because He healed me, I can see that I had been dead inside—I had been the walking dead until Jesus restored me back to life.

I am in several online post-abortion groups. Over and over, I read posts saying, "No one told me I would feel like this." Women and men are uninformed about the effects of abortion on themselves.

Some women are writing their stories of abortion regret. You'll find Tori Shaw and Serena Dyksen, for example in the Resources.

Men are beginning to speak out, too, about the effects of abortion on them. They self-report that they have experienced:

- Becoming violent
- Abusing alcohol
- Abusing drugs
- Isolating themselves from others
- Resisting authority
- Realizing their difficulty in bonding with women and children[c]

Over 50 billion known abortions have been performed in the U.S. since 1973. That's 50 billion women just in the U.S. walking through life like the walking dead, their vitality drained away.

---

a   Psalm 51:11
b   Psalm 51:12
c   Guy Condon and David Hazard, *Fatherhood Aborted* (Carol Stream, IL: Tyndale House Publishers, 2001).

Thirty-six percent[a] of post-abortive women or over 18 billion go to church at least once per month. But what about the men who got them pregnant?

Zombies have no regard for life, they have no idea they are dead, and they want to infect others so that others also become zombies.

That was me. I had no regard for life. I voted only pro-choice, I volunteered for a pro-choice organization that raised funds to support pro-choice politics, and I counter-protested Christians who prayed in front of an abortion facility. I was defending what I chose, all the while not knowing that I was walking through life dead inside.

When you see celebrities shout their abortions, remember that they are defending what they chose.[b]

If we want to end abortion, then we need to heal our people so that they *do* regard life, they are restored to life themselves, and they stop spreading zombie-ism. Imagine 18 billion women shouting their abortion regret!

"Cry loudly, do not hold back;
Raise your voice like a trumpet,
And declare to My people their transgression
And to the house of Jacob their sins. (Isaiah 58:1 NASB)

I shout my abortion regret! I cry loudly. I do not hold back. I raise my voice like a trumpet and declare my transgressions and my sins to God's people.

I call for post-abortive women and men to join me and so many others in raising our voices like a choir of trumpets!

---

a   Care-Net, "Study of Women Who Have Had an Abortion & Their Views on Church" (PDF, 2016).
    Go to resources.care-net.org/free-resources to get a copy.
b   Read "Listen to Alyssa Milano" cherylkrichbaum.blog/2019/08/22/listen-to-alyssa-milano and "Busy Philipps' Fallacy" cherylkrichbaum.blog/2020/03/11/busy-philipps-fallacy on my blog.

Accepting God's Prodigals

If God can restore King David and still call him a man after God's own heart,[a] then God can restore post-abortive women and men.

We Christians, as representatives of our God who desires the return of His prodigal children, must be ready to welcome women and men with open arms.

Here is Jesus' parable that we call "The Prodigal Son":

> *"There was a man who had two sons. And the younger of them said to his father, 'Father, give me the share of property that is coming to me.' And he divided his property between them.*
>
> *"Not many days later, the younger son gathered all he had and took a journey into a far country, and there he squandered his property in reckless living. And when he had spent everything, a severe famine arose in that country, and he began to be in need, so he went and hired himself out to one of the citizens of that country, who sent him into his fields to feed pigs. He was longing to be fed with the pods that the pigs ate, and no one gave him anything.*
>
> *"But when he came to himself, he said, 'How many of my father's hired servants have more than enough bread, but I perish here with hunger! I will arise and go to my father.'*
>
> *"And he arose and came to his father. But while he was still a long way off, his father saw him and felt compassion, and ran and embraced him and kissed him.*
>
> *"And the son said to him, 'Father, I have sinned against heaven and before you. I am no longer worthy to be called your son.'*
>
> *"But the father said to his servants, 'Bring quickly the best robe, and put it on him, and put a ring on his hand, and shoes on his feet. And bring the fattened calf and kill it, and let us eat and celebrate. For this my son was dead, and*

---

a   1 Samuel 13:14; Acts 13:22

112

is alive again; he was lost, and is found.' And they began to celebrate.

"But his older brother was angry and refused to celebrate."[a]

Notice that although the prodigal left and squandered his inheritance, his father did not deny their father-child relationship. Often, post-abortive women and men exclude themselves from our Christian family. Sometimes they won't go to a local church. Sometimes they go to a local church but won't get involved, most often excluding themselves from children's ministry.

Also notice that the brother was angry that the prodigal was reconciled to the family. Unfortunately, there are many Christians who treat the post-abortive in such a way that they don't want to go to a local church.

That was not the experience for me, but I did have an experience of feeling that my testimony was not to be shared publicly. The first two times that I told my story of God's goodness despite my abortion, my Christian audience did not know how to respond to me. As a result, I felt like I got the Christian cold shoulder. It wasn't until I wrote my memoir that I realized that they just didn't know how to respond to me, so I forgave them.

> *Many post-abortive women exclude themselves from God' forgivenss, won't go to church, or won't serve at their church.*

You too may not know how to respond to someone's abortion story. Even I have responded with shock rather than obvious agape love, and I had to apologize to my friend. We can, however, prepare ourselves to respond well. Let's gather some ideas from the father in Jesus' parable.

When the father saw his prodigal son, he felt compassion and embraced him,[b] so let's ask for permission to give the other person

---

a   Luke 15:11-18a, 20-24, 28 ESV
b   Luke 15:20

a hug. Thank the person for trusting you with her or his story. Ask her or him how they think God feels about their choice and about them today. Kindly refer them to your local post-abortion healing groups. When the person is ready, offer to pray. If the person has acknowledged her or his sin and feels restored to the joy of salvation, celebrate![a]

From now until you encounter post-abortive women or men, let us pray for their restoration because Jesus came for sinners[b] and because restored people do not promote abortion.

---

a   Luke 15:24
b   Luke 5:32

Post-Abortion Healing Resources

The inclusion of the following resources does not imply their endorsement of this book.

Contact your local church to see what they offer for post-abortion healing or consider the resources below.

For Women

Surrendering the Secret

Surrendering the Secret is a study that offers an 8-step biblical healing modeled by women who have been where you are. The study is designed to bring women together who understand the need for seeking peace with the past and desire a better understanding of God's plan for making the most painful losses of our past work for His glory! SurrenderingTheSecret.com

Forgiven and Set Free

Linda Cochrane. *Forgiven and Set Free: A Post-Abortion Bible Study for Women*, Baker Books, 2015, Grand Rapids, MI.

Celebration of Restoration

The Celebration of Restoration luncheon was birthed from the idea of one woman reaching across the table to another, sharing a message of healing and coming together to celebrate God's peace and forgiveness.

For Men

Healing a Father's Heart

Linda Cochrane and Kathy Jones. *Healing a Father's Heart: A Post-Abortion Bible Study for Men*. Baker Books, 1996, Grand Rapids, MI.

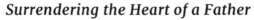

Surrendering the Heart of a Father

Patricia Layton and Mike Layton. *Surrendering the Heart of a Father: A Man's Guide to Abortion Recovery*, 2020. For the complete program, go to SurrenderingTheSecret.com

For Women and Men

Pregnancy Resource Centers

Most pregnancy resource centers offer post-abortion healing. Find the resource center near you.

Care-Net provides a directory of centers in the U.S. Care-Net.org/find-a-pregnancy-center

Heartbeat International provides a directory of centers around the world. HeartbeatInternational.org/worldwide-directory

Deeper Still

Deeper Still hosts weekend healing retreats for both women and men who have experienced or participated in an abortion as the mother or father of the child. GoDeeperStill.org

Rachel's Vineyard

Rachel's Vineyard weekends for healing after abortion are offered throughout the year in locations across the United States and Canada, with additional sites around the world. Rachel's Vineyard is a ministry of Priests for Life. RachelsVineyard.org

SaveOne

Abortion has a deep ripple effect. You may have chosen abortion personally, lost a child to abortion, or your life has been profoundly affected by abortion. SaveOne can help you through the healing process. SaveOne.org

Post-Abortive Women

Some of the following post-abortive women offer healing classes, but I pray that all of them will inspire you.

Abby Johnson, And Then There Were None

Abby Johnson has always been fiercely determined to help women in need. This desire is what led Abby to a career with Planned Parenthood, our nation's largest abortion provider, and caused her to flee the organization, becoming an outspoken advocate for the pro-life movement. AbbyJohnson.org @AbbyJohnson

Cheryl Krichbaum, MybodyMyworship

Award-winning author, speaker, and creator of The Missing Sex Ed Lessons. Cheryl equips Christians to compassionately reach the abortion-minded and to value the sanctity of sex. CherylKrichbaum.blog @MybodyMyworship MybodyMyworship.com

Jenna Stringer, Present Reality

Present Reality aids post-abortive women in need of emotional and spiritual support and provides resources for abortion-minded women and families who are facing crisis pregnancies. Jenna, currently married with six children, regrettably had two abortions but is now committed to presenting the reality of abortion and the severe consequences that come along with what pro-aborts call "choice." Facebook.com/JennaPostAbortive

Julie Mad-Bondo, Julie's Heart Cry

Julie's Heart Cry is a faith-based organization that aims to eliminate obstacles that otherwise might lead women to choose an abortion both locally and globally. We hope to establish birthing centers in developing countries in order to come alongside women who are grieving from abortion, miscarriage, or the loss of a child. JuliesHeartCry.org

Serena Dyksen, She Found His Grace Ministry

She Found His Grace is Serena's personal testimony of coming from poverty, rape at 13, abortion, and being abandoned to finding God's grace, love, healing, and freedom. SerenaDyksen.com @SheFoundHisGrace

Tori Shaw, Not Forgotten Ministries

Not Forgotten Ministries knows the unalterable value of every life is given by God at the moment He created it. We are devoted to ending abortion, helping post-abortive mothers find healing, and offering a place for pre-born babies to be honored. facebook.com/TheyAreNotForgotten

Suggested Prayers

Day 22

What's your worship song or hymn for today?_____

What's your posture of worship for today?

☐ dancing/giddying   ☐ prostrating   ☐ giving thanks
☐ praising in song/hymn   ☐ kneeling   ☐ confessing
☐ singing/making music   ☐ serving God

Psalm 34:3-5, 51:1-4, 7-8, 10-14; Proverbs 6:17, Hebrews 4:12

Lord, reconcile post-abortive women and men with You for while they keep silent about their sin, their bodies waste away through their groaning, which we may see as anger, bitterness, or depression. You teach us in Deuteronomy 28 and Leviticus 26 that we'll receive blessings when we live in commitment to You but consequences when we don't. Even through C.S. Lewis' *The Lion, the Witch, and the Wardrobe*, we know that there were laws on which this earth was built.

May billions of women and men soon recognize that their vitality has drained away because they have shed innocent blood. But may they also understand that because of Your great compassion, they can be cleansed from their guilt and purified of their sins, just as You have cleansed and purified me. May they no longer be haunted because they have done evil in Your sight but instead be renewed with joy and loyalty to You.

May all Christians confess their rebellion and then joyfully sing of Your forgiveness. Lord, bring billions into Your loving and healing arms. Thank You for making all of us whiter than snow!

Prayer for 40 Days for Life

Lord, thank You for equipping sidewalk counselors to speak life to women and men who have chosen abortion before and are about to choose it again. May Your sword of the Spirit discern thoughts and attitudes of the heart.

Take Up Your Sword of the Spirit

J esus, the Word,[a] open my mind to understand the Scriptures.[b]

Swords and Words

Matthew 4:1-11

After Jesus was baptized, He was led by the Holy Spirit into the wilderness. He fasted for 40 days and 40 nights. Not surprisingly, He was hungry.

Satan came to Him and said, "If You are the Son of God, command that these stones become bread."

Jesus answered, "It is written, 'Man shall not live by bread alone but by every word that proceeds from the mouth of God.'"[c]

Satan took Jesus into the holy city, set Him on the pinnacle of the temple, and said, "If You are the Son of God, throw Yourself down. For it is written: 'He shall give His angels charge over

---

a   John 1:1
b   Luke 24:45
c   Deuteronomy 8:3

you,"[a] and 'In their hands they shall bear you up lest you dash your foot against a stone.'"[b]

Jesus responded, "It is written, 'You shall not tempt the Lord your God.'"[c]

Satan took Jesus up on an exceedingly high mountain and showed Him all the kingdoms of the world and their glory. He said, "All these things I will give You if You will fall down and worship me."

Jesus responded, "Away with you, satan! For it is written, 'You shall worship the Lord your God, and Him only you shall serve.'"[d]

Satan left Him, and angels came to minister to Him.

Swords

Short Swords

On "Day 1" of this book, Joan of Arc took up the short sword and said, "Work through me, Lord, to defeat every enemy that dares to get close enough. I am on a mission, and I will not be deterred," which is based on Ephesians 6:17:

> *And take the helmet of salvation, and the sword of the Spirit, which is the word of God. (NASB)*

The transliteration of the Greek word for sword, in these verses, is *machaira*—a short sword or dagger. This type of sword is the same type of sword referenced in Hebrews 4:12:

---

a   Psalm 91:11
b   Psalm 91:12
c   Deuteronomy 6:16
d   Deuteronomy 6:13, 10:20; Joshua 24:14

For the word of God is living and active and sharper than any two-edged sword and piercing as far as the division of soul and spirit, of both joints and marrow, and able to judge the thoughts and intentions of the heart. (NASB)

Short swords were used by Roman soldiers who were on the front lines. They are better for thrusting and for stabbing over and under shields in close combat.

Long Swords

In contrast, the Apostle John saw a long sword coming out of Jesus' mouth as recorded in Revelation:

I saw one like a son of man, clothed in a robe reaching to the feet, and girded across His chest with a golden sash. His head and His hair were white like white wool, like snow; and His eyes were like a flame of fire. His feet were like burnished bronze, when it has been made to glow in a furnace, and His voice was like the sound of many waters.

In His right hand He held seven stars, and out of His mouth came a sharp two-edged sword; and His face was like the sun shining in its strength. (Revelation 1:13b-16 NASB, emphasis mine)

The transliteration of the Greek word for sword in Revelation 1:17 is *rhomphaia*—a long sword. Craftsman added more decorative elements to long swords because they were carried by commanders, who led and inspired their troops. In battle, the longer blade reached past the enemy's weapon.

Word

Curiously, Greek also has more than one way to express the word *word*—the sword of the Spirit, which is the *word* of God. In

Ephesians 6:17, the transliterated Greek word for *word* is *rhema*. Rhema is also in Matthew 4:4:

> But He answered and said, "It is written, 'Man shall not live by bread alone, but by every word that proceeds from the mouth of God.' " (NKJV)

However, the Apostle John uses the Greek word *logos* to describe Jesus:

> In the beginning was the Word, and the Word was with God, and the Word was God. (John 1:1 NASB)

Logos

Logos had a twofold use in Ancient Greece—speech (or a message) and reason. Aristotle taught three modes of persuasion: ethos, pathos, and logos.[a] Of logos, he said, "Persuasion is effected through the speech itself when we have proved a truth or an apparent truth by means of the persuasive arguments suitable to the case in question."[b] That is to say that Aristotle taught his students to use logos to provide reasons—logic—to support a thesis.

From this we can understand that Jesus, who is logos, is Himself the message of God and the reason for salvation.

Rhema

In contrast, *rhema* is an utterance rather than a prepared message. Where *logos* is a prepared speech, *rhema* is an impromptu statement. *Logos* is to long sword as *Rhema* is to short sword.

Ideally, the sword of the Spirit in Ephesians 6:17 is allowing the Holy Spirit to speak through us. However, not all of us are

---

a Aristotle. *Rhetoric,* trans. W. Rhys Roberts (New York: The Modern Library, 1954), 23.

b Aristotle, 25.

practiced in surrendering to the Holy Spirit. We can practice surrendering to the Holy Spirit, and I encourage you to do so.

Allowing the Holy Spirit to speak through us often becomes easier when we have studied the Bible. Whether we have verses memorized word-for-translated-word or not, scripture comes out of us more often when we know what scripture says. Then we can use it as Jesus did when He was tempted by the devil.[a]

In the rest of this guide, I continue to provide you with suggested prayers. However, I encourage you to read the Bible passages yourself then allow the Holy Spirit to speak through you as you pray.

Praying through Agape Love

Remember to imagine yourself as a worship warrior, suited up for battle, then worship and pray through the agape love of God's heart for *all* people.

People in the pro-choice—or pro-abortion—movement often evoke anger in us for their lack of compassion for pre-born babies they cannot see, for their blindness to the devastation to our society, and for their illogical reasoning. For many of us, we respond in anger with our own illogical arguments.

However, the Lord does not call us to respond in anger, no matter how righteous that anger may be. Jesus said:

> *"I say to you who hear, love your enemies, do good to those who hate you, bless those who curse you, pray for those who mistreat you." (Luke 6:27-28 NASB)*

You may say that Jesus was flippin' mad in the temple. However, the Bible does not *say* that Jesus was mad; it does show us that Jesus made His point about people using His Father's house of prayer for making money.[b] When Jesus flipped tables, He did so

---

a   Matthew 4:1-11
b   Matthew 21:12-13, Mark 11:15-18

because profiteers were distracting His people *from* God rather than attracting His people *to* Him.

Getting mad at unbelievers is different than flipping tables manned by Christian profiteers. We need to remember that Jesus was kind to all but the priests and scribes because He wanted to bring people into relationship with God. (He was blunt with the priests and scribes because they were supposed to be leading His people well but weren't.) Likewise, we need to be kind to people who disagree with us because we want them to be in relationship with Christ.

> *Be kind to people who disagree with you so that they will be attracted to Christ.*

If you do know of a church that is profiting from or promoting abortions, then pray before you flip tables to make a point! Otherwise, be kind to people who disagree with you so that they will be attracted to Christ.

Whether you consider yourself an evangelical or not, consider this: If people truly understood who they are in Christ, then they wouldn't choose abortion—even further, they wouldn't choose extramarital sex, which accounts for about 84% of abortions in the U.S.

> *If I speak with the tongues of men and of angels, but do not have love, I have become a noisy gong or a clanging cymbal. (1 Corinthians 12:1 NASB)*

Let's choose not to be noisy gongs or clanging cymbals. Instead, let's choose to be someone who attracts people to God through His agape love.

> *Let all that you do be done in love. (1 Corinthians 16:14 NASB)*

> *Owe nothing to anyone except to love one another; for he who loves his neighbor has fulfilled the law. For this, "You shall not commit adultery, You shall not murder, You shall not steal,*

You shall not covet," and if there is any other commandment, it is summed up in this saying, "You shall love your neighbor as yourself." Love does no wrong to a neighbor; therefore, love is the fulfillment of the law. (Romans 13:8-10 NASB)

So, as those who have been chosen of God, holy and beloved, put on a heart of compassion, kindness, humility, gentleness and patience; bearing with one another, and forgiving each other, whoever has a complaint against anyone; just as the Lord forgave you, so also should you. Beyond all these things put on love, which is the perfect bond of unity. Let the peace of Christ rule in your hearts, to which indeed you were called in one body; and be thankful. (Colossians 3:12-15 NASB)

Anyone who claims to be in the light but hates a brother or sister is still in the darkness. (1 John 2:9 NASB)

Do not repay anyone evil for evil. Be careful to do what is right in the eyes of everyone. If it is possible, as far as it depends on you, live at peace with everyone. *Do not take revenge, my dear friends, but leave room for God's wrath, for it is written: "It is mine to avenge; I will repay," says the Lord. On the contrary: "If your enemy is hungry, feed him; if he is thirsty, give him something to drink. In doing this, you will heap burning coals on his head." Do not be overcome by evil, but overcome evil with good. (Romans 12:17-21 NASB, emphasis mine)*

Resources

The inclusion of the following resources does not imply their endorsement of this book. You'll find a consolidated list of resources on page 175.

Pro-Life Bible Verses

The best pro-life verses are in the New Testament, but you'll find pro-life bible verses from both the Old and New Testaments listed at MybodyMyworship.com/best-pro-life-bible-verse.html

More Verses to Pray for Someone's Salvation

You'll find many more Bible verses to pray for someone's salvation, in "Cheryl's Contending List" in the appendix of *ReTested: The Story of a Post-Abortive Woman Called to Change the Conversation.*

Pregnancy Resource Centers in the U.S.

Care-Net provides a directory of centers in the U.S. Care-Net.org/find-a-pregnancy-center

Pregnancy Resource Centers Around the World

Heartbeat International provides a directory of centers around the world. HeartbeatInternational.org/worldwide-directory

Pro-Women's Healthcare Centers in the U.S.

The mission of the consortium of **Pro Women's Healthcare Centers (PWHC)** is to partner with women to provide comprehensive, convenient, compassionate, high-quality medical services and access to social services that empower them to care for their health. Refer a woman in crisis or find a center for your own healthcare, which not only benefits your own health but also supports the mission of the pro-life healthcare center. PWHCenters.org

U.S. Abortion Facility Inspection Reports

Check My Clinic is a comprehensive database of health and safety violations at abortion facilities. CheckMyClinic.org

Former Abortion Workers

And Then There Were None (ATTWN) is a registered nonprofit organization that exists to help abortion clinic workers leave the abortion industry. ATTWN is pro-life without exceptions. While we believe in and wholeheartedly support all peaceful pro-life efforts, ATTWN seeks to end abortion from the inside out. AbortionWorker.com

Pro-Life in Central and East Africa

Learn about supporting life in Central and East Africa through **Julie's Heart Cry**, a faith-based organization that aims to eliminate obstacles that otherwise might lead women to choose an abortion both locally and globally. JuliesHeartCry.org

Suggested Prayers

Day 23

What's your worship song or hymn for today?_____

What's your posture of worship for today?

☐ dancing/giddying   ☐ prostrating   ☐ giving thanks
☐ praising in song/hymn   ☐ kneeling   ☐ confessing
☐ singing/making music   ☐ serving God

Ephesians 4:17-24, 6:14; John 4:7-45, 8:1-11, 17:20-23

Lord, The Church often feels divided—so many denominations, so many interpretations of scripture, so many divisive words and actions. Lord, I plead with You to unite us as one body with Jesus as our head. Knit us together to acknowledge You so that we no longer walk as the unbelieving world in ignorance and hardness of heart.

Remove our calluses and soften our hearts to unite under Your headship, to make known Your love and compassion, especially for those with multiple spouses like Jesus did with the woman at the well and for those caught in extramarital sex like Jesus did with the woman caught in adultery.

Let us not give ourselves over to sensuality for the practice of every kind of impurity and greediness but instead be examples of the agape love and warmth that Your light provides, for we are a bright light in the world.

Renew our minds. May we daily put on our new selves in the likeness of You. May the world recognize the righteousness (not self-righteousness) and holiness (not holier-than-thou) of the truth belted around our waists.

Prayer for 40 Days for Life

Lord, thank You for the 40 Days for Life worship warriors who stand firm shoulder-to-shoulder no matter their denominational beliefs. We stand with them.

Day 24

What's your worship song or hymn for today?_____

What's your posture of worship for today?

☐ dancing/giddying   ☐ prostrating   ☐ giving thanks
☐ praising in song/hymn   ☐ kneeling   ☐ confessing
☐ singing/making music   ☐ serving God

Psalm 139:13–15

Lord, Creator, thank You for forming my innermost parts, for knitting me together in my mother's womb. I give thanks and praise to You because I am reverently and wonderfully made. Wonderful are Your works, and I am so grateful that I am one of them. My soul knows it very well. My frame was not hidden from You when I was being formed in secret and intricately and skillfully formed as if embroidered with many colors.

Lord, lift the veil from the eyes of the abortion-minded, including those who have had an abortion or who pressured a woman to have an abortion, to know that they, too, are reverently and wonderfully made by You, intricately and skillfully formed and loved by You. Show them their own value as well as the value of all pre-born babies. Open their hearts to valuing all life, their own and others', whether pre-born or already born.

Prayer for 40 Days for Life

Lord, thank You for the sidewalk counselors who see Your beautiful creations choosing death for Your beautiful creations. We mourn with You and with sidewalk counselors.

Lord, keep us all hopeful for Your salvation coming to the abortion-minded, post-abortive, and abortion workers.

Day 25

What's your worship song or hymn for today?_____

What's your posture of worship for today?

- ☐ dancing/giddying
- ☐ praising in song/hymn
- ☐ singing/making music
- ☐ prostrating
- ☐ kneeling
- ☐ serving God
- ☐ giving thanks
- ☐ confessing

Hebrews 3:13, 5:2, 12:5, 12:15–16; Ezekiel 36:26–27

Lord, the feminist movement has changed from asking for equality in work and pay to bitterness. We apologize for any part we had in allowing the root of bitterness to sprout. So many hearts have been poisoned by this suppressed anger. Our hearts are broken over women feeling like they are not loved by us or by You.

Lord, show compassion to those who are ignorant of Your ways and stray from them. Show us how to be compassionate ourselves.

Lord, give us and the abortion-minded new hearts and new spirits. Remove our hearts of stone and give us hearts of flesh. Thank You for putting Your Spirit within us and in the abortion-minded, causing us all to walk in Your ways.

We do not underestimate the value of Your discipline and training. We choose not to get depressed when You correct us but instead sing praise songs and hymns in all circumstances, choosing to surrender all to You and Your ways.

Lord, we choose to encourage each other to not be stubborn or hardened by sin's deceitfulness. Show us how to encourage someone today.

Lord, we watch over each other to make sure that no one misses the revelation of Your grace. We watch for the root of bitterness and when we see it, we choose to forgive rather than suppress our anger because bitterness only causes trouble and poisons the hearts of many.

Lord, thank You for reminding us to keep each other accountable so that no one among us lives in sexual immorality, becoming careless about Your blessings.

Prayer for 40 Days for Life

Lord, thank You for encouraging sidewalk counselors. May they choose hope in You rather than anger for women, abortion workers, or anyone else who supports abortion overtly or out of ignorance. Thank You for protecting their hearts from bitterness.

Day 26

What's your worship song or hymn for today?_____

What's your posture of worship for today?

- ☐ dancing/giddying
- ☐ prostrating
- ☐ giving thanks
- ☐ praising in song/hymn
- ☐ kneeling
- ☐ confessing
- ☐ singing/making music
- ☐ serving God

John 3:16-18, Matthew 28:19-20, 1 John 5:13

Lord, You have given us the commission of making disciples, but many of us are not yet disciples ourselves. Lord, make us like Jesus for that's what it means to be Your disciple. Lord, as we become more and more like You, show us who to help become disciples as well.

Lord, there are specific people in our lives whom we want in our Christian family. We call out to You, asking that You lift the veils that cover their eyes and soften their hearts to believe in Your agape love. For them, we pray specifically:

You, God, so loved _____ that You gave Your only begotten Son, that _____ believes in Christ and does not perish but has eternal life. For You did not send Your Son to _____ to judge _____ but that _____ might be saved through Christ. _____ believes in Jesus and is not judged. _____ believes in the name of the only begotten Son of God. _____ is Your disciple, and I will teach him/her Your ways.

Lord, we pray also for all the abortion-minded: All those who are unsure about abortion or who promote abortion believe in the name of the Son of God so that they know that they have eternal life and value the lives that You created.

Lord, send Your Holy Spirit to soften unbelieving hearts to believe, believing hearts to become disciples, and disciples' hearts to seek Your plan and purpose for their lives. Lord, open hearts all around the world to follow all of Your ways.

Prayer for 40 Days for Life

Lord, thank You for the disciples at abortion facilities around the world and their willingness to spreading Your gospel of love. Protect them from every kind of evil.

Day 27

What's your worship song or hymn for today?_____

What's your posture of worship for today?
- ☐ dancing/giddying
- ☐ prostrating
- ☐ giving thanks
- ☐ praising in song/hymn
- ☐ kneeling
- ☐ confessing
- ☐ singing/making music
- ☐ serving God

Psalm 127:3, Isaiah 44:24, Genesis 1

Lord, first soften the heart of all Christians and church-goers to believe that children are a heritage from You, that the fruit of the womb is a reward, not a burden. Soften the hearts of the abortion-minded to believe that they were formed in the womb by You, the Creator Who loves them. Then do the same for those who do not yet know You.

Lord, starting with Christians, give all people a deep-seeded confidence that You formed us in the womb. You are the maker of all things. You stretched out the heavens by Yourself. You spread out the earth all alone. You are the Creator and all things made by You are good.

Lord, change the hearts of the abortion-minded to fully believe that children are a heritage from You, that the fruit of the womb a reward.

Prayer for 40 Days for Life

Lord, thank You for reminding sidewalk counselors that You made all those who support, promote, and commit abortions and that You love them despite their sins. Thank You for desiring that all come to righteousness. Lord, protect the hearts and minds of the 40 Days for Life worship warriors.

Day 28

What's your worship song or hymn for today?_____

What's your posture of worship for today?
- ☐ dancing/giddying
- ☐ prostrating
- ☐ giving thanks
- ☐ praising in song/hymn
- ☐ kneeling
- ☐ confessing
- ☐ singing/making music
- ☐ serving God

Job 32:8, John 3:6, Romans 8:16, Luke 11:13, Galatians 5:22-23

Lord, it's through Your Spirit that we understand. Thank You for giving me more of the Holy Spirit and for making the fruit of the Spirit evident in me—fruit of love, joy, peace, patience, kindness, goodness, faithfulness, gentleness, and self-control.

Lord, I ask that You also give more of the Holy Spirit to my (spouse, children, parents, siblings, nieces and nephews, friends, coworkers, church). Increase the fruit of the Spirit within us and increase our understanding of Your ways.

Lord, increase the Holy Spirit and the light around every woman who is considering abortion right now. Shed light on the way out of the darkness that surrounds her. Put Christ followers in her path. Save her babies from death and save her from darkness and lead her and her child to everlasting life.

Prayer for 40 Days for Life

Lord, increase the Holy Spirit in the 40 Days for Life worship warriors. Make their light even brighter. Give them more fruit of the Holy Spirit, most especially peace that passes understanding.

Day 29

What's your worship song or hymn for today?_____

What's your posture of worship for today?

☐ dancing/giddying   ☐ prostrating   ☐ giving thanks
☐ praising in song/hymn   ☐ kneeling   ☐ confessing
☐ singing/making music   ☐ serving God

Romans 12:1-2; Ephesians 5:28-33, 6:4; Philippians 4:13

Lord, I give my body to You because of all You have done for me. Let me be a living and holy sacrifice—the kind You find acceptable. It's my body and with it I choose to worship You!

I will not copy the behaviors and customs of this world but instead allow You to transform me into a new person by changing the way I think. Thank You for teaching Your will for me—Your good, pleasing, and perfect will.

Lord, thank You for all the men who follow You and Your ways. Thank You that their example of loving their wives, future wives, and former wives like Christ agape loves The Church is evident to all the world. Lord, thank You for all the men who bring up children in discipline and instruction of the Lord.

Lord, thank You for all the women who follow You and Your ways. Thank You for their example of respecting their husbands, future husbands, and former husbands in response to agape love just as we respect You in response to Your agape love for us. Lord, thank You for all the women who bring up their children in discipline and instruction of the Lord.

May the world know we are Christians by our agape love.

Prayer for 40 Days for Life

Lord, thank You for the 40 Days for Life worship warriors for their choice to be a living sacrifice. Thank You for opening their minds to Your will for them. Give them strength as they do all things through Christ.

Day 30

What's your worship song or hymn for today?_____

What's your posture of worship for today?

☐ dancing/giddying   ☐ prostrating   ☐ giving thanks
☐ praising in song/hymn   ☐ kneeling   ☐ confessing
☐ singing/making music   ☐ serving God

Matthew 5:44-45, Titus 3:2-7, Romans 12:18, Exodus 17:12

Lord, I am choosing to love my enemies: I love abortion facility workers, post-abortive women and men, and pro-abortion and pro-choice women and men—even the politicians. I bless all of them whether they curse me or not. I will do good to those who hate me.

I pray for all those who spitefully use me and persecute me. Their words do not hurt me because I am Your child. You, the all powerful One, make the sun rise and the rain fall on the evil and the good, on the just and on the unjust. I trust in You to bring justice.

Lord, thank You for reminding me to never tear down anyone with my words but instead to be considerate, humble, and courteous to everyone. I choose to do all things in love and in Your strength, choosing peace as far as it depends on me.

I remember that I have been easily led astray as a slave to worldly passions and pleasures, behaving foolishly in my own stubborn disobedience. However, Your extraordinary compassion and Your love that overpowered me is the brightness that can overcome others, even those who disagree with me. Thank You for your extravagant mercy.

Prayer for 40 Days for Life

Lord, thank You for reminding sidewalk counselors to be strong and courageous as You stand with them, as do we. You will not fail them or abandon them. Remind them to do all things in love and in Your strength, choosing peace as far as it depends on them.

We hold up the 40 Days for Life worship warriors, as Aaron and Hur held up Moses' hands, so that they are steady.

Day 31–32

Give

J esus, Holy Servant,[a] open my mind to understand the Scriptures.[b]

Sowing Purposefully
Matthew 25:14-30

Before traveling to India for business, an English lord called his servants: Fearless, Faithful, and Faltering. The lord entrusted them with his assets.

To Fearless, he gave five talents. To Faithful, he gave two talents. To Faltering, he gave one talent. Then the lord left for his travels.

Fearless traded the five talents and made another five, totaling ten. Faithful traded the two talents and made another two, totaling four. Faltering buried the one talent.

When the lord returned, Fearless gave the ten talents to his lord, who said, "Well done, good and faithful servant. You were

---

a   Acts 4:30
b   Luke 24:45

dependable with a few things. I will make you ruler over many things. Enter the joy of your lord."

Faithful gave the four talents to his lord, who said, "Well done, good and faithful servant. You were dependable with a few things. I will make you ruler over many things. Enter the joy of your lord."

Faltering gave the one talent to his lord, who said, "You lazy servant. You knew that I reap where I have not sown and gather where I have not scattered seed. You should have deposited my assets with the bankers so that I would have received it back with interest. Give that talent to Fearless! For to all who have, more will be given, and they will have abundance, but from those who do not invest, what they have will be taken away."

As servants of our Lord, let us be fearless and faithful to sow our talent, time, and treasure into the lives that He knit together—mothers, fathers, and pre-born babies.

Sowing our Talent, Time, and Treasure

When we lived in Minneapolis, I went with my church to volunteer at a food pantry, sorting donations. When we moved to Georgia, I volunteered at a food pantry in the next county, about 20 minutes from my home, sorting donations and helping clients to shop for their needs. When pastors from two different churches started a food pantry in the town where we lived, I helped them get started by developing a marketing campaign to solicit donations.

For the first two pantries, I sowed my time and my treasure through donations. For the third pantry, I sowed my talent and my treasure.

When we moved to Virginia, my boys and I toured the local food pantry, but I was disappointed in how they served people, so I did not sow my talent, time, or treasure.

A few years later at the grocery store, the clerk asked if I'd like to donate to the local food pantry. "No, thank you," I said.

"Why?" my teen asked. "You volunteered for the food pantry in Georgia."

I responded, "Do you remember that we took a tour of this pantry shortly after we moved here?"

You can be choosy about which organizations you sow into.

"Yeah," he said.

"Do you remember that we saw them giving food but not doing anything to help their clients get up and out of their need?"

"Yeah," he said.

"The food pantries we supported in Georgia and Minnesota not only gave out food, but they helped their clients budget, find financial assistance, and write resumes. This place doesn't do any of that," I explained. "They also took *faith* out of their name, so Christ is no longer part of what they do."

I heard the grocery clerk say, "Hmm" quietly and nod her head. The next time we went shopping, we bought items for a food pantry that's further away but helps its clients get up and out of their need.

I share my experiences with food pantries not to brag but to illustrate that you can be choosy about which organizations you sow into. You can also sow into organizations not just with your treasure but also your time and your talent.

If our hearts are for saving babies and their parents from abortion, then our talent, time, and treasure should reflect that. Jesus said,

"For where your treasure is, there your heart will be also."
(Matthew 6:21 NASB)

Sowing **talent** means doing projects that we are especially qualified to do. For me, that means leading post-abortion healing classes through my local Christian pregnancy resource center, authoring books like this one, writing social media posts, and speaking wherever I'm invited.

Sowing **time** means doing projects that need to be done, even though they may not be particularly interesting. For me, that means collecting diapers from friends and neighbors and delivering them to my local Christian pregnancy resource center.

Sowing **treasure** means sending money. Even though making money is not one of my talents, I do donate to my local Christian pregnancy resource center. I started with just a few dollars per month. Later, I was able to increase that monthly amount. And even though I'm not a big donor, I go to the annual banquet, invite my friends to join me, and donate an additional amount. Whether it's a few dollars each month or several times that amount, any money is better than no money to serve families who are vulnerable to abortion.

Time
Talent
Treasure
Sow wisely.

Let us make a habit of intentionally sowing our talent, time, and treasure where God leads us.

> *"Do not store up for yourselves treasures on earth, where moth and rust destroy, and where thieves break in and steal. But store up for yourselves treasures in heaven, where neither moth nor rust destroys, and where thieves do not break in or steal; for where your treasure is, there your heart will be also." (Matthew 6:19-21 NASB)*

Social Media

Sometimes I will sow my time into social media, engaging pro-choice women. Once, a woman said, "Name your local pregnancy resource center. I bet you can't do it without looking it up."

"Mosaic," I responded immediately. I didn't get a response from her, but I was impressed that she knew such places exist because many women do not. (Look up yours using the directories listed in the Resources section.)

Do you know why she challenged me? Because women in the pro-choice movement can spot a hypocrite in two seconds flat.

> They'll know we are Christians by our love, by our love.
> Yes, they'll know we are Christians by our love.

I remember singing this in church when I was young. My dad, the choir director, would pull it out regularly. A Catholic Priest named Fr. Peter Scholtes wrote the hymn in the 1960s. He was inspired by Jesus' words at the Last Supper:

> "A new commandment I give to you, that you love one another, even as I have loved you, that you also love one another. By this all men will know that you are My disciples, if you have love for one another." (John 13:34-35 NASB)

Let us prove to the pro-choice movement that we are loving by being the hands and feet of Jesus, sowing seeds of God's agape love so that we may reap a harvest of saved babies and saved mothers and fathers.

Do not be deceived, God is not mocked; for whatever a man sows, this he will also reap. For the one who sows to his own flesh will from the flesh reap corruption, but the one who sows to the Spirit will from the Spirit reap eternal life. Let us not lose heart in doing good, for in due time we will reap if we do not grow weary. So then, while we have opportunity, let us do good to all people, and especially to those who are of the household of the faith. (Galatians 6:7-10 NASB)

Time and Talent Ideas

Here are a few ideas of how you can sow your time or your talent.

AmazonSmile

Use AmazonSmile and set your non-profit to your local Christian pregnancy resource center.

AmazonSmile is a simple way for you to support your favorite charitable organization every time you shop, at no cost to you. When you shop at `smile.amazon.com`*, you'll find the exact same low prices, vast selection and convenient shopping experience as Amazon.com, with the added benefit that Amazon will donate 0.5% of your eligible purchases to the charitable organization of your choice. You can choose from over one million organizations to support.*[a]

Simple Support

- Host a fundraiser campaign to support your local pregnancy resource center. Many centers have simple

---

a   Amazon, "About AmazonSmile," accessed July 1, 2020, `https://smile.amazon.com/about`.

campaigns in which they provide empty baby bottles to fill with loose change.

- Support your local pregnancy resource center in another way. If you're good at social media, ask if they need someone to create posts. If you're a talented photographer, ask if they need someone to photograph babies and parents. If you are a website developer, ask if they need someone to help with their website. If you paint well, ask if they need someone to paint their center. If you know how to organize events, ask if they need someone to organize a 5k fun run fundraiser. Recently, I met a woman who has a jewelry business. She sells jewelry to raise money for a maternity home for unwed teens![a] What is your talent? God designed you with talents. Have you buried them? Dig them up and invest them wisely!

- Join the next **40 Days for Life** campaign to pray at your local abortion facility.

Church

If you're a leader at your church, consider this: as many as 25% of the women in your congregation may have had an abortion, and we have no statistics on the men who got them pregnant. If they have not been through a post-abortion healing program, then they are most likely wounded.

If you want to lead your congregation into the battle against abortion—or any other justice or evangelical issue—then you need spiritually healthy warriors. If you're building a spiritual army, you need to prepare your warriors. Are your warriors spiritually healthy or wounded?

Host post-abortion healing, or partner with your local pregnancy resource center, which most likely leads post-abortion healing groups.

---

a   On Facebook, search for Blooming for Life.

Here are some additional ideas to consider:

- Make sure both women and men know how to contact the local pregnancy resource center and know what services they offer.

- If you offer classes, include studies on the sanctity of life and the sanctity of sex. (Contact MybodyMyworship for curriculum.)

- Host Embrace Grace parenting classes to provide a bridge from the local pregnancy resource center to your church so that you can mentor new parents in their walk to become disciples.

- And here's an out-of-the-box idea: Revise your membership statement to include agreement on the sanctity of life and the sanctity of sex.

Post-Abortive Women and Men

If you are post-abortive and healed, you can:

- Lead post-abortion healing classes for your local Christian pregnancy resource center or your church.

- Host a Celebration of Restoration luncheon. (See the Resources section for information about this event.)

- Share social media posts by post-abortive women, such as Julie's Heart Cry, Serena Dyksen, or me, Cheryl Krichbaum.

- Meet with your youth pastor, young adult pastor, or the pastor who ministers to couples, offering to speak at their meetings.

Resources

The inclusion of the following resources does not imply their endorsement of this book.

40 Days for Life

40 Days for Life is an internationally coordinated 40-day campaign that aims to end abortion locally through prayer and fasting, community outreach, and a peaceful all-day vigil in front of abortion businesses. 40DaysForLife.com

Celebration of Restoration Luncheons

The Celebration of Restoration luncheon was birthed from the idea of one woman reaching across the table to another, sharing a message of healing, and coming together to celebrate God's peace and forgiveness. OurChoiceOurVoice.org

Embrace Grace

The non-profit Embrace Grace, Inc. equips churches on how to love and support the single and pregnant young women in their communities. EmbraceGrace.com

Pregnancy Resource Centers in the U.S.

Care-Net provides a directory of centers in the U.S. Care-Net.org/find-a-pregnancy-center

Pregnancy Resource Centers throughout the World

Heartbeat International provides a directory of centers around the world. HeartbeatInternational.org/worldwide-directory

Pro-Women's Healthcare Centers

The mission of the consortium of Pro Women's Healthcare Centers (PWHC) is to partner with women to provide comprehensive, convenient, compassionate, high-quality medical services and access to social services that empower them to care for their health. Refer a woman in crisis or find a center for your own healthcare, which not only benefits your health but also supports the mission of the pro-life healthcare center. PWHCenters.org

Heather Hobbs

Heather Hobbs is a pro-life speaker, advocate for life, rape survivor, domestic violence activist, wife to an amazing husband, and mother of four. She focuses on the so-called "hard" cases as she was urged and pressured by medical doctors to abort three of her four children. HeatherHobbs.org @HeatherHobbsHumanRights

Former Abortion Workers

And Then There Were None (ATTWN) is a registered nonprofit organization that exists to help abortion clinic workers leave the abortion industry. ATTWN is pro-life without exceptions. While we believe in and wholeheartedly support all peaceful pro-life efforts, ATTWN seeks to end abortion from the inside out. AbortionWorker.com

Cheryl Krichbaum

Cheryl Krichbaum is an award-winning author, speaker, and creator of The Missing Sex Ed Lessons. Cheryl equips Christians to compassionately reach the abortion-minded and to value the sanctity of sex. CherylKrichbaum.blog @MybodyMyworship MybodyMyworship.com

Jenna Stringer

Present Reality aids post-abortive women in need of emotional and spiritual support and provides resources for abortion-minded women and families who are facing crisis pregnancies. Jenna, currently married with six children, regrettably had two abortions but is now committed to presenting the reality of abortion and the severe consequences that come along with what pro-aborts call "choice." Facebook.com/JennaPostAbortive

Julie Mad-Bondo

Learn about supporting life in Central and East Africa through **Julie's Heart Cry**, a faith-based organization that aims to eliminate obstacles that otherwise might lead women to choose an abortion both locally and globally. JuliesHeartCry.org

Serena Dyksen

She Found His Grace is Serena's personal testimony of coming from poverty, rape at 13, abortion, and being abandoned to finding God's grace, love, healing, and freedom. SerenaDyksen.com @SheFoundHisGrace

Tori Shaw

Not Forgotten Ministries knows the unalterable value of every life is given by God at the moment He created it. We are devoted to ending abortion, helping post-abortive mothers find healing, and offering a place for pre-born babies to be honored. facebook.com/TheyAreNotForgotten

Suggested Prayers

Day 31

What's your worship song or hymn for today?_____

What's your posture of worship for today?

☐ dancing/giddying   ☐ prostrating   ☐ giving thanks
☐ praising in song/hymn   ☐ kneeling   ☐ confessing
☐ singing/making music   ☐ serving God

Proverbs 21:13, Matthew 18:30-34, 1 John 3:17, James 2:13

Lord, do I shut my ear to the cry of the poor? Do I close my heart against those who are in need? Search my heart and know me, Lord. Your love abides in me. Show me how to show love and mercy to those in need, especially women and men with crisis pregnancies. What do You want me to offer—my talent? my time? my treasure? and through which pro-life organization?

Lord, today I will find out which is the nearest Christian pregnancy resource center and learn what services they offer. I will take a tour and thank those who work there personally. If You are calling me to support the center through my talent, time, or treasure, I will obey You and give. I know that You honor every minute and every penny that I give.

Prayer for 40 Days for Life

Lord, thank You for the 40 Days for Life worship warriors who are giving their time to pray for Your creation—the abortion-minded and their babies. Protect the talent, time, and treasure of Your worship warriors from the thief, who comes to steal, kill, and destroy.

Day 32

What's your worship song or hymn for today?_____

What's your posture of worship for today?

- ☐ dancing/giddying
- ☐ praising in song/hymn
- ☐ singing/making music
- ☐ prostrating
- ☐ kneeling
- ☐ serving God
- ☐ giving thanks
- ☐ confessing

Matthew 25:37-40, Hebrews 12:28, 1 Peter 4:10-11

Lord, when did I see You hungry and feed You or thirsty and give You something to drink? When did I see You as a stranger and invite You in? When did I clothe You? When did I see You sick or in prison and come to You?

Lord, I offer You worship with my whole body with reverence and awe. In humbleness, I choose to serve others.

Lord, make me known in heaven as the one who served the least of them for Your glory and not my own.

Prayer for 40 Days for Life

Lord, thank You for the sidewalk counselors around the world who see strangers every day and invite them into Your loving arms. Protect their minds from discouragement and give them peace that passes understanding.

Day 33

Raise Them in the Way They Should Go

J esus, Head of The Church,[a] open my mind to understand the Scriptures.[b]

Taking the Promised Land

Deuteronomy 6:7-8, Isaiah 54:1-3a, Matthew 28:19-20

"Repeat these commands, these decrees, these regulations again and again," Moses said. "Talk about them when you are at home or when you are driving to your after-school activities. Talk about them during breakfast and at bedtime. Put signs on your doors and your walls. Put scripture in your email signature. Post Bible verses on social media regularly. Wear bracelets, baseball caps, or—Cheryl's favorite—t-shirts!

"I gave these commands to your parents who were Egyptian slaves, and now I'm repeating them for you who are free and about to start a new way of life in the Promised Land. I cannot

a   Ephesians 1:22
b   Luke 24:45

join you in the Promised Land, so it is now your responsibility to keep the Word alive."

The above was, of course, a dramatization of Moses' words recorded in Deuteronomy 6:7-8:

> *Repeat them (commands, decrees, and regulations per verse 1) again and again to your children. Talk about them when you are at home and when you are on the road, when you are going to bed and when you are getting up. Tie them to your hands and wear them on your forehead as reminders. (NLT)*

Teach Them

When I was in Uganda, the Pearl of Africa, I saw these signs posted on the walls of an elementary school:

> *Abstain from sex until you get married.*
>
> *Have self-control in sexual matters.*
>
> *Avoid alcohol. It affects you.*
>
> *School is a chance. Make use of it.*
>
> *Body changes are never a sign to start sex.*
>
> *Respect and appreciate your teachers.*
>
> *Say, "No" to gifts.*
>
> *Avoid walking in dark places.*
>
> *AIDS kills.*
>
> *AIDS has no age limit.*

Following your faith can help you to abstain.

Avoid situations where you might be raped.

The woman who was giving us the tour was watching quietly as I took pictures of each sign. I could almost read her mind: *Why is this American so interested in posters about sex?* So I said to her, "You don't see signs like these in the United States, not even for the older kids."

Her demeanor changed. In an almost indignant response, she said, "Why not? These children need to know!"

She was right, of course. We cannot talk about abortion without talking about extramarital sex. Our children—and teens, young adults, and even senior citizens—need to know what extramarital sex and abortion do to women and men, young and not-so-young, from a scientific perspective, a social perspective, and definitely a biblical perspective. Any perspective that we know, we need to share.

Everyone born since 1955 in the U.S. has known legal abortion their entire adult lives.

Realize that what Moses said was not just for people with children. God's ways are for everyone, so we need to share them with everyone, whether they are our biological children or not.

God even talks specifically to women who have never had biological children, saying that they will have more children than those who gave birth.

> *"Woman, be happy! You have not had any children, but you should be very happy. Yes, the woman who is alone will have more children than the woman with a husband." This is what the Lord says. "Make your tent bigger. Open your doors wide. Don't think small! Make your tent large and strong because you will grow in all directions. (Isaiah 54:1-3a ERV)*

Think about who your spheres of influence are. Coworkers? Nieces and nephews? Those in your crafting group? Friends shooting hoops?

When Jesus told the disciples to go make disciples, He said to spread the word in Jerusalem first, then Judea and Samaria (a wider circle), and then the rest of the world. We always need to start with those who are closest to us and then "make our tent bigger."

> *Jesus said, "but you will receive power when the Holy Spirit has come upon you; and you shall be My witnesses both in Jerusalem, and in all Judea and Samaria, and even to the remotest part of the earth." (Acts 1:8 NASB)*

Jesus' Great Commission is recorded in several places in the Bible,[a] but we most often quote the very end of Matthew:

> *And Jesus came up and spoke to them, saying, "All authority has been given to Me in heaven and on earth. Go therefore and*
>
> 1. *make disciples of all the nations,*
>
> 2. *baptizing them in the name of the Father and the Son and the Holy Spirit,*
>
> 3. *teaching them to observe all that I commanded you;*
>
> *and lo, I am with you always, even to the end of the age." (Matthew 28:18-20 NASB)*

Let's take a closer look at the words *disciples*, *nations*, and *teaching*. I'm purposely skipping over baptizing because every denomination has their own beliefs about baptism and getting into that discussion does not help us be worship warriors united in the abortion battle.

---

a   Mark 16:15, Luke 24:46-47, Acts 1:8

Disciples

Sometimes we mistakenly equate *disciple* with *believer*. A *believer* is someone who believes that Jesus is the Son of God and the last sacrifice for her or his own sins.[a] We usually refer to believers as Christians, but let's remember that we got the name Christians from pagans.[b]

Jesus did not call us *Christians* or tell us to make *Christians*. He called us *disciples* and told us to make *disciples*.

Here is my favorite description of a *disciple*:

> *"Do you understand what it means to be someone's disciple?"*
>
> *... "I thought it meant 'student.'"*
>
> *"Yes, but not how you think of it. You're thinking of Y'shua [Jesus] like an algebra teacher. But to be a disciple means more than learning. It means to become like your teacher. It means transformation from what I am into what my teacher is. Y'shua said once, 'Everyone who is fully trained will be like his teacher.'"*
>
> *... "You would eat when I eat, you would rest when I rest, and under the same olive tree. You wouldn't take the shortcut while I went the long way. We would be inseparable. You would live like my shadow, mimicking my actions until you could do what I do without thinking, until you had the same instincts, thoughts, and words."[c]*

Leading people to choose Christ is great! But it's just the beginning. We cannot leave them there. We must help them to continue to grow, becoming more and more like Jesus. They need to become more like Jesus and so do you.

---

a Hebrews 10:12

b Acts 11:26

c Matt Mikalatos. *Imaginary Jesus*. (Carol Stream, IL: Tyndale House Publishers, 2010), 44.

Nations

The word *nations* in Matthew 28:19 is the Greek word *ethnos*, which is the basis of our English words *ethnic* and *ethnicity*. In today's English, *nation* refers to geopolitical boundaries on a map; whereas, biblical *ethnos* refers to people groups, who share kinship and cultural traditions.

Remember that the geopolitical boundaries we have today are very different than when Jesus spoke His Great Commission. The U.S., of course, did not exist! Today, the U.S. is a modern-day nation full of ethnicities.

Abortion is a world-wide pandemic even in countries where it is illegal.

If you are called to be a missionary whether short-term or long, then go! While there, teach the sanctity of life and the sanctity of sex for abortion is a world-wide pandemic even in countries where it is illegal. (You can learn about my experience teaching the sanctity of life and of sex as a short-term missionary in chapter 10 of *ReTested.*)

If you're not called to be a missionary, then guide those in your spheres of influence right where you are. As Jill Briscoe said, "You go where you're sent, and you stay where you're put, and you give what you've got."

Generational Influence

Think about your spheres of influence. Do you see tweens, teens, or young adults regularly? How about adults?

Yes, other adults. We must influence all generations because everyone born in 1955 or later has known legal abortion in the U.S. all of their adult lives, so abortion is "normal" for us. Grandmothers advocate for abortion for their granddaughters because they were caught up in the women's rights movement of the 1960s and 70s.[a]

---

a   See Grandmothers for Reproductive Rights
    GrandmothersForReproductiveRights.org

If abortion is ever to be rare or ended completely, then we have to reeducate everyone about both abortion and extramarital sex.

The thought of teaching scares many people. You may be thinking, *I'm not a teacher! I don't have the gift of teaching!* However:

- We teach when we talk.
- We teach when we post on social media with agape love.
- We teach when we share social media posts with agape love.
- We teach when we bring abortion and sex ed into a conversation.

Just by having a conversation, we are teaching what God has to say and why His way benefits us rather than restricts us.

Here are some ideas:

- You can start by telling people what you're learning while reading this book. Find a video on my YouTube channel (@MybodyMyworship) or someone else's and use it to ask people what they think. Engage them in conversation.
- Invite people to your home to discuss what abortion does to women and men spiritually. (You can share my videos[a] or read my website[b] and then discuss as a group.)
- If you have tweens, teens, or "not marrieds" in your family, enroll them in one of *The Missing Sex Ed Lessons* online courses (go to MybodyMyworship.com for a list of course offerings).
- Get a group together to learn biblical sex education. (See if your local pregnancy resource center offers a class.)
- When you're having coffee with a friend, talk about what you've learned about abortion and be sure to mention that there are many post-abortion healing programs. They may

---

a   "Biblical Reasons for the Sanctity of Life" on YouTube @MybodyMyworship youtu.be/9j_hsoooiDg
b   "Spiritual Effects of Abortion" MybodyMyworship.com/spiritual-effects-of-abortion.html

or may not be post-abortive, but you'll be surprised at how many friends admit they're post-abortive once they see that you are lovingly talking about it.

Social Media

When we post politicized abortion news on social media, we preach to the choir and alienate those who don't like a particular political party. That's not what I'm suggesting you do. Skip the politics and stick to the bible, research, and testimony.

> *Let all that you do be done in love. (1 Corinthians 16:14 NASB)*

We do not end abortion by making it illegal—just ask the people of Uganda where abortion is illegal yet prevalent. If Roe v Wade and Doe v Bolton were overturned today, abortion would go underground. We'd have a new illegal drug trade. We'd have another precursor to a second civil war.

We end abortion by changing hearts.

---

*We do not end abortion by making it illegal.
We end abortion by changing hearts.*

Resources

The Missing Sex Ed Lessons

Faith- and science-based courses that equip tweens, teens, and unmarried adults to delay sexual encounters so that they avoid STIs, crisis pregnancies, and challenging relationships. These online courses provide positive, empowering, pro-life sex education completed in the privacy of your own home.

MybodyMyworship.com

Suggested Prayer

Day 33

What's your worship song or hymn for today?_____

What's your posture of worship for today?

- ☐ dancing/giddying
- ☐ praising in song/hymn
- ☐ singing/making music
- ☐ prostrating
- ☐ kneeling
- ☐ serving God
- ☐ giving thanks
- ☐ confessing

Deuteronomy 6:7, James 1:5, Titus 2:2-8

Lord, You say that we should teach your ways diligently to our children. Lord, whisper to me how I should teach the children You gave me, whether they are grown or are my coworkers or nieces and nephews or others in my community.

Make me a model to children as a life nobly lived. Make me authentic in my integrity. Show me how to teach the clear, wholesome message that cannot be condemned.

I may not feel qualified to teach or know what to say, but You do! Tell me who are the children You gave me to teach and teach me how to instill Your ways in them. Show me how to teach them in my house (or a coffee shop), when we are traveling, when it's time to sleep, and when it's time to rise. I need Your wisdom, Lord. Show me the way.

Prayer for 40 Days for Life

Lord, thank You for equipping sidewalk counselors to teach your ways diligently to the women and men You introduce to them. Thank You for protecting sidewalk counselors from evil every day.

Be the Light of the World

J esus, King of kings,[a] open my mine to understand the scriptures.[b]

Let It Shine

Matthew 5:13-16

"You got out the electric candle! I love how it flickers like a real candle. So calming." I slipped upstairs to get Grandmother's quilt and my book. Then I quietly reentered the candlelit room, but it was dark.

"What happened to the candle?" I asked.

"Hmm? Oh, I put a basket over it."

"The candle is still on but under a basket?"

"MmmHmm."

"Why would you light a lamp and then put it under a basket? Put it up high so that it lights up the house!"

---

a   Revelation 17:14

b   Luke 24:45

"Nor do they light a lamp and put it under a basket, but on a lamp stand and it gives light to all who are in the house." (Matthew 5:15 NKJV)

—ɷ—

"Daniel, look!"
"Huh? What? Oh, wow! Is that Seattle?"
"Look at all those lights! So beautiful against the darkness."
"I read that Seattle is a city on a hill. So is Rome."
..."and Jerusalem!"

"A city that is set on a hill cannot be hidden." (Matthew 5:14b NKJV)

Jesus is the Light.[a] When we believe that He died for our sins, He lives in us, so His light is in us. He said:

"You are the light of the world.... Let your light shine before others that they may see your good works and give glory to your Father in heaven." (Matthew 5:14a, 16 NRSV)

Think about the light in a room. With light, we can see even in the darkness.

Sources of light provide warmth. Campfires, for example, provide warmth in the cool night air. People gather around campfires to make food, eat, and enjoy each other's company. How are we like campfires? Are people attracted to our light and our warmth? Do they see God more clearly because they are near us?

---

a   John 1:5

After returning from my first trip to Uganda, I became more intentional about making people smile. Why? Because Pastor Cyrus Mad-Bondo pointed out that we may be the only Christians others meet. We want them to have a pleasant experience so that they want to be around Christians. I took that lesson home and now try to be a Jesus light to others here, too.

I encourage you to be purposeful in letting your light shine so brightly that others notice and want The Light, too. When people see your light, they are more likely to listen to your reasoning.

You laid aside the deeds of darkness by working through Days 6-17. Now let's put on our armor of light and stand firm, attracting people to the warmth of God's Light found within us.

Therefore let us lay aside the deeds of darkness and put on the armor of light. (Romans 13:1b NASB)

Suggested Prayer

Day 34

What's your worship song or hymn for today?_____

What's your posture of worship for today?

- ☐ dancing/giddying
- ☐ prostrating
- ☐ giving thanks
- ☐ praising in song/hymn
- ☐ kneeling
- ☐ confessing
- ☐ singing/making music
- ☐ serving God

Job 31:15, Matthew 5:14-16

Lord, loving my enemies in the abortion battle is hard. I need Your eyes to see them as You see them. I know in my head that You made me in the womb and that You fashioned them in their mothers' wombs, too. Help the eyes of my heart to know this truth and to radiate Your light no matter how I feel so that others will see The Light and want it for themselves.

Prayer for 40 Days for Life

Lord, thank You for giving sidewalk counselors the strength to love their enemies and see them as You see them. Thank You for strengthening the light in the 40 Days for Life worship warriors, so the abortion-minded can see Your way out of the darkness and into Your glorious freedom.

Day 35

What's your worship song or hymn for today?_____

What's your posture of worship for today?

☐ dancing/giddying   ☐ prostrating   ☐ giving thanks
☐ praising in song/hymn   ☐ kneeling   ☐ confessing
☐ singing/making music   ☐ serving God

Ephesians 4:14-16, 2 Timothy 1:6, Matthew 28:19-20

Lord, use me to reach luke-warm Christians for Your glory. Fan the flame inside of me to make what I have in You attractive to others. Bring me people to influence so that we, The Church, would no longer be children tossed to and fro, carried about with every wind of doctrine, the trickery of others, or cunning craftiness of deceitful plotting. Make those of us who are believers into disciples. Convince our hearts that Your way is the best way because You designed and created the world.

Use me to speak the truth in love to all ethnicities near and far. You, Jesus, are the Word—be the words in my mouth. Grow us, The Church, from childhood into adulthood in You, Who is the head of The Church body.

Join and knit us together, so that we may effectively work together, everyone doing their share, causing the growth of The Church body for the educating of ourselves and others in love.

Prayer for 40 Days for Life

Lord, give particular insight to sidewalk counselors of women and men who know Jesus but don't know He's pro-life. Give them the right words at the right time to speak Your love with grace and mercy.

Day 36

What's your worship song or hymn for today?_____

What's your posture of worship for today?

- ☐ dancing/giddying
- ☐ praising in song/hymn
- ☐ singing/making music
- ☐ prostrating
- ☐ kneeling
- ☐ serving God
- ☐ giving thanks
- ☐ confessing

Matthew 5:14, 1 Thessalonians 4:1-8, Luke 11:13, Galatians 5:22-23

Lord, open the eyes of those around me to see Your Holy Spirit living in me. I am the light of the world. Let others use that light in order to see the love, joy, peace, patience, kindness, goodness, faithfulness, gentleness, and self-control that Your Holy Spirit produces in me. Make others attracted to the light that You put in me so that they choose You and choose to control their own bodies, living a holy life themselves. Soften hearts to Your love shown through me and other Christians so that holiness spreads throughout our country and the world.

Prayer for 40 Days for Life

Lord, open the minds of all those who see the 40 Days for Life worship warriors to see Your Holy Spirit and the fruit of the Spirit in them. Make others attracted to their light so that they choose You and Your ways, which are good for them and their babies. Soften hearts to Your love shown through the 40 Days for Life campaign.

Day 37

What's your worship song or hymn for today?_____

What's your posture of worship for today?

- ☐ dancing/giddying
- ☐ praising in song/hymn
- ☐ singing/making music
- ☐ prostrating
- ☐ kneeling
- ☐ serving God
- ☐ giving thanks
- ☐ confessing

Deuteronomy 6:6, 8-9; Matthew 28:19-20

Lord, I commit myself wholeheartedly to Your ways. I am tying them to my hands and wearing them on my forehead as reminders. I am writing them on my doorpost and on my gates.

Lord, You have commissioned me to make disciples. Who do You want me to reach? Show me how to teach them to follow Your ways. Thank You for being with me always.

Prayer for 40 Days for Life

Lord, thank You for being with the 40 Days for Life worship warriors always. Thank You for reminding them to wear Your ways on their foreheads, doorposts, and gates. Thank You for protecting them, their families, and their property from all kinds of evil.

Day 38

What's your worship song or hymn for today?_____

What's your posture of worship for today?

- ☐ dancing/giddying
- ☐ praising in song/hymn
- ☐ singing/making music
- ☐ prostrating
- ☐ kneeling
- ☐ serving God
- ☐ giving thanks
- ☐ confessing

Matthew 5:13-16

Lord, I am the salt of the earth—don't ever let me lose my flavor. I am the light of the world. Like a city that is set on a hill, I cannot be hidden. Like a lamp on a lamp stand, I give light to all who are in my home. Thank You for filling me with the Holy

Spirit more and more each day so that Your light in me shines before other people who see Your work through me and glorify You for what they see.

Prayer for 40 Days for Life

Lord, thank You for the saltiness and bright light of the 40 Days for Life worship warriors. Thank You for shining the Light brightly before others, that they would glorify You.

Day 39

What's your worship song or hymn for today?_____

What's your posture of worship for today?
- ☐ dancing/giddying
- ☐ prostrating
- ☐ giving thanks
- ☐ praising in song/hymn
- ☐ kneeling
- ☐ confessing
- ☐ singing/making music
- ☐ serving God

Philippians 2:14-15, James 1:5

Lord, remind me today and everyday to do everything You ask without murmuring or questioning Your wisdom so that I prove blameless and honest, innocent and pure—Your child and heir without blemish—in the midst of a morally crooked and spiritually perverted generation, among whom I am seen as a bright light, a beacon shining out clearly in the world of darkness.

Prayer for 40 Days for Life

Lord, give the 40 Days for Life worship warriors wisdom and remind them to ask You for wisdom in the midst of the morally crooked and spiritually perverted abortion facilities where the worship warriors are seen as a bright light, a beacon shining clearly in the darkness.

Day 40

What's your worship song or hymn for today?_____

What's your posture of worship for today?
- ☐ dancing/giddying
- ☐ praising in song/hymn
- ☐ singing/making music
- ☐ prostrating
- ☐ kneeling
- ☐ serving God
- ☐ giving thanks
- ☐ confessing

Isaiah 58:1; Acts 2, 4:4, 8:1, 1 Thessalonians 5:14-24

Lord, give me Your loving words to speak boldly, like Peter spoke on Pentecost. Show me how and where to speak the truth in love. Use our voices to bring thousands into Your Church. Send Your Holy Spirit to do mighty works in the hearts of women and men who do not know You or understand Your ways. May they hear Your agape love through me.

Lord, show me which Christians to influence. Show me how to comfort the fearful and support those who lack confidence in their walk. Thank You for giving me patience for everyone. Remind me to stand firm in loving people who disagree with me and encouraging others to do the same while continuously pursuing what is Your good will for all of our society and for the world.

Lord, I will rejoice always, pray continually, and give thanks to You in all circumstances. I will follow the Holy Spirit's leading rather than quench it. I will hold on to what is good and reject every kind of evil. Lord, thank You for being the God of peace who sanctifies me through and through. I commit to keeping my whole spirit, soul, and body blameless. Thank You for being faithful to me.

Prayer for 40 Days for Life

Jesus, thank You for being the Prince of Peace, leading the worship warriors at abortion facilities around the world through battles each day, helping them to stand firm with feet fitted for peace. Thank You for rallying Your troops to be brave, to speak boldly, and love abundantly.

Acknowledgments

Thank you to Dick Rabil for your beautiful cover design and all the beautiful designs that we didn't choose. Your work is stellar!

Thank you to Erin Voorheis for your perspective, your research assistance, and your editing skills.

Thank you to Andrew Towler for re-introducing me to King Jehoshaphat's story.

Thank you to Katharine, Margaret, Dick, Kathi, Ellie, Tanya, Anne Marie, Caneel, Christine, Gina, Adam, Amy, Gail, Will, and Meredith for lifting me up and helping me understand my calling.

Thank You to my Lord and Savior for guiding me through every step of writing this book and the booklet before it in such a short time frame. Your will be done. May You be glorified in all You instructed me to write.

Consolidated List of Resources

The inclusion of the following resources does not imply their endorsement of this book.

40 Days for Life

40 Days for Life is an internationally coordinated 40-day campaign that aims to end abortion locally through prayer and fasting, community outreach, and a peaceful all-day vigil in front of abortion businesses. 40DaysForLife.com

Crisis Pregnancy Resources

U.S. Pregnancy Resource Centers

Care-Net
Care-Net is a 501(c)3 nonprofit organization that empowers women and men considering abortion to choose life for their unborn children and find abundant life in Christ. Care-Net provides a directory of Christian pregnancy resource centers, many of which also provide post-abortion healing, at resources.Care-Net.org/find-a-pregnancy-center

LoveLine
LoveLine, a ministry started by Abby Johnson, connects with women in crisis, actively listening to hear their needs. They

commit to caring and following through to ensure their most critical needs are met first. They provide ongoing support in the woman's own community through loving volunteers and organizations with which they have a relationship. LoveLine.com

International Pregnancy Resource Centers

Heartbeat International
Heartbeat International is the first network of pro-life pregnancy resource centers founded in the U.S. (1971), and it is now the most expansive network in the world. Heartbeat has over 2,800 affiliated pregnancy help locations including pregnancy help medical clinics (with ultrasound), resource centers, maternity homes, and adoption agencies in more than 60 countries around the world to provide alternatives to abortion. Heartbeat International provides a directory of Christian pregnancy resource centers, many of which also provide post-abortion healing, at HeartbeatInternational.org/worldwide-directory

Bahamas Godparent Center
The Bahamas Godparent Center is a pregnancy, youth and family resource under the umbrella of ProLife Bahamas, the 1st Pro Life organization in the Bahamas. BahamasGodParentCenter.org

U.S. Abortion Facility Inspection Reports

Check My Clinic
Check My Clinic is a comprehensive database of health and safety violations at abortion facilities. CheckMyClinic.org

Pro-Women's Healthcare Centers
The mission of the consortium of Pro Women's Healthcare Centers (PWHC) is to partner with women to provide comprehensive, convenient, compassionate, high-quality medical services and access to social services that empower them to care for their health. Refer a woman in crisis or find a center for your own healthcare, which not only benefits your own health but also supports the mission of the pro-life healthcare center. PWHCenters.org

Embrace Grace

The non-profit Embrace Grace, Inc. equips churches on how to love and support the single and pregnant young women in their communities. EmbraceGrace.com

Post-Abortion Recovery Support

Contact your local church to see what they offer for post-abortion healing or consider the resources below.

For Women

Surrendering the Secret
Surrendering the Secret is a study that offers an 8-step biblical healing modeled by women who have been where you are. The study is designed to bring women together who understand the need for seeking peace with the past and desire a better understanding of God's plan for making the most painful losses of our past work for His glory! SurrenderingTheSecret.com

Forgiven and Set Free
Linda Cochrane. *Forgiven and Set Free: A Post-Abortion Bible Study for Women*, Baker Books, 2015, Grand Rapids, MI.

For Men

Healing a Father's Heart
Linda Cochrane and Kathy Jones. *Healing a Father's Heart: A Post-Abortion Bible Study for Men.* Baker Books, 1996, Grand Rapids, MI.

Surrendering the Heart of a Father
Patricia Layton and Mike Layton. *Surrendering the Heart of a Father: A Man's Guide to Abortion Recovery*, 2020. For the complete program, go to SurrenderingTheSecret.com

For Women and Men

Pregnancy Resource Centers
Most pregnancy resource centers offer post-abortion healing. Find the resource center near you.

Care-Net provides a directory of centers in the U.S. `Care-Net.org/find-a-pregnancy-center`

Heartbeat International provides a directory of centers around the world. `HeartbeatInternational.org/worldwide-directory`

Deeper Still
Deeper Still hosts weekend healing retreats for both women and men who have experienced or participated in an abortion as the mother or father of the child. `GoDeeperStill.org`

Rachel's Vineyard
Rachel's Vineyard weekends for healing after abortion are offered throughout the year in locations across the United States and Canada, with additional sites around the world. Rachel's Vineyard is a ministry of Priests for Life. `RachelsVineyard.org`

SaveOne
Abortion has a deep ripple effect. You may have chosen abortion personally, lost a child to abortion, or your life has been profoundly affected by abortion. SaveOne can help you through the healing process. `SaveOne.org`

Celebration of Restoration
The Celebration of Restoration luncheon was birthed from the idea of one woman reaching across the table to another, sharing a message of healing, and coming together to celebrate God's peace and forgiveness. `OurChoiceOurVoice.org`

Post-Abortive Women Who Are Now Pro-Life

After the Abortion Photography Series by Angela Forker

After the Abortion Photography Series helps people to see the pain and devastation that often follows abortion while also helping post-abortive men and women find forgiveness and healing through Jesus. The goal of these photos is threefold:

1. Pregnant women will want to avoid this pain and guilt and instead choose life (and that the fathers and grandparents will rise up to the occasion and not pressure the woman to abort her baby).

2. Christians will see that they need to respond to post-abortive women with love and compassion.

3. Post-abortive women will find forgiveness and healing through Jesus.

aftertheabortion.com (Follow on Facebook, too!)

Abby Johnson, And Then There Were None

Abby Johnson has always been fiercely determined to help women in need. This desire is what led Abby to a career with Planned Parenthood, our nation's largest abortion provider, and caused her to flee the organization, becoming an outspoken advocate for the pro-life movement. AbbyJohnson.org @AbbyJohnson

Cheryl Krichbaum, MybodyMyworship

Award-winning author, speaker, and creator of The Missing Sex Ed Lessons. Cheryl equips Christians to compassionately reach the abortion-minded and to value the sanctity of sex. CherylKrichbaum.blog @MybodyMyworship MybodyMyworship.com

Jenna Stringer, Present Reality

Present Reality aids post-abortive women in need of emotional and spiritual support and provides resources for abortion-minded women and families who are facing crisis pregnancies. Jenna,

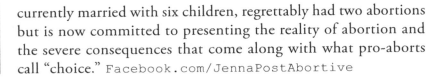

currently married with six children, regrettably had two abortions but is now committed to presenting the reality of abortion and the severe consequences that come along with what pro-aborts call "choice." Facebook.com/JennaPostAbortive

Julie Mad-Bondo, Julie's Heart Cry

Julie's Heart Cry is a faith-based organization that aims to eliminate obstacles that otherwise might lead women to choose an abortion both locally and globally. We hope to establish birthing centers in developing countries in order to come alongside women who are grieving from abortion, miscarriage, or the loss of a child. JuliesHeartCry.org

Serena Dyksen, She Found His Grace Ministry

She Found His Grace is Serena's personal testimony of coming from poverty, rape at 13, abortion, and being abandoned to finding God's grace, love, healing, and freedom. SerenaDyksen.com @SheFoundHisGrace

Tori Shaw, Not Forgotten Ministries

Not Forgotten Ministries knows the unalterable value of every life is given by God at the moment He created it. We are devoted to ending abortion, helping post-abortive mothers find healing, and offering a place for pre-born babies to be honored. facebook. com/TheyAreNotForgotten

Abortion Survivors

Abortion Survivors Network

The Abortion Survivors Network (ASN) is the only advocacy and support group for abortion survivors and their families world-wide. AbortionSurvivors.org

Carrie Fischer

Pro-life author, speaker, and blogger. facebook.com/ CarrieFischerSpeaker

Jennifer Milbourn

Jennifer Milbourn, vacuum-aspiration abortion survivor, equips Christians to forgive others so that they are free to live their purpose. "In every situation you encounter, always choose life!" facebook.com/Jennifer-Milbourn-Vacuum-Aspiration-Abortion-Survivor

Former Abortion Workers

And Then There Were None

And Then There Were None (ATTWN) is a registered nonprofit organization that exists to help abortion clinic workers leave the abortion industry. ATTWN is pro-life without exceptions. While we believe in and wholeheartedly support all peaceful pro-life efforts, ATTWN seeks to end abortion from the inside out. AbortionWorker.com

Special Needs Babies

Precious Baby Project by Angela Forker

The Precious Baby Project raises awareness for babies with special needs, showing the world that EVERY baby is beautiful and has value. Angela's prayer is that people would see these photos and choose life and affirm others who choose life, even when their baby might have a frightening diagnosis. preciousbabyphotography.com/precious-baby-project

Books

Condon, Guy and David Hazard. *Fatherhood Aborted*. Carol Stream, IL: Tyndale House Publishers, 2001.

Krichbaum, Cheryl. *ReTested: The Story of a Post-Abortive Woman Called to Change the Conversation*. OH: Author Academy Elite, 2019.

McElhinney, Ann and Phelim McAleer. *Gosnell: The Untold Story of America's Most Prolific Serial Killer.* Washington, DC: Regnery Publishing, 2018.

Abortion History

An outline of abortion history is at MybodyMyworship.com/history-of-abortion.html

Bible Verses on Sanctity of Life & Sanctity of Sex

The best **pro-life verses** are in the New Testament, but you'll find pro-life bible verses from both the Old and New Testaments listed at MybodyMyworship.com/best-pro-life-bible-verse.html

Bible verses on **sexual immorality** are listed at MybodyMyworship.com/bible-verses-on-sexual-immorality.html

Hymns, Worship & Praise Music

Find a list of **worship hymns** and add your own suggestions at MybodyMyworship.com/worship-hymns.html

Find a list of **praise and worship songs** that focus on God and add your own suggestions at MybodyMyworship.com/praise-and-worship-songs.html

Sex Ed Courses

The Missing Sex Ed Lessons

Faith- and science-based courses that equip tweens, teens, and unmarried adults to delay sexual encounters so that they avoid STIs, crisis pregnancies, and challenging relationships. These online courses provide positive, empowering, pro-life sex education completed in the privacy of your own home. MybodyMyworship.com

About the Author

Cheryl Krichbaum is a prayer warrior turned worship warrior! Her passion for restoring people to God's beautiful plan is not just for pre-born babies, but also for women in crisis and the men who got them pregnant.

Using her training in audience analysis and her experience as a post-abortive woman, she provides insight into reaching the pro-choice for life and for Christ through God's agape love. She desires love, joy, and peace that passes understanding for all people, and she's determined to reach them like Jesus did—with truth spoken in love.

Cheryl's award-winning memoir, *ReTested: The Story of a Post-Abortive Woman Called to Change the Conversation*, tells her own story of restoraion and of worshiping God in all circumstances.

In addition to writing, Cheryl is a speaker and the designer of *The Missing Sex Ed Lessons* online courses "because we can't talk about abortion without talking about sex."

Cheryl lives near Washington, DC with her husband, their two teens, and her mom. She travels back to her home state of Minnesota regularly to dip her toes in one of its many rivers (and maybe a lake, too) and to give her Dad a big hug.

Connect with Cheryl at MybodyMyworship.com and @CherylKrichbaum.

BRING CHERYL INTO YOUR CHURCH OR ORGANIZATION

Millions of post-abortive women and men are in The Church.

Millions more should be in The Church but aren't—yet.

And unless we teach all that Christ commanded about the sanctity of life and the sanctity of sex in our own local churches, millions more Christians will abort. Let's not let that happen on our watch.

Instead, let's end abortion first in our own churches, then in the communities we serve—both locally and internationally.

Invite Cheryl to encourage and equip your group or congregation to share the love of Christ with the post-abortive and the abortion-minded.

Contact Cheryl:
MybodyMyworship.com

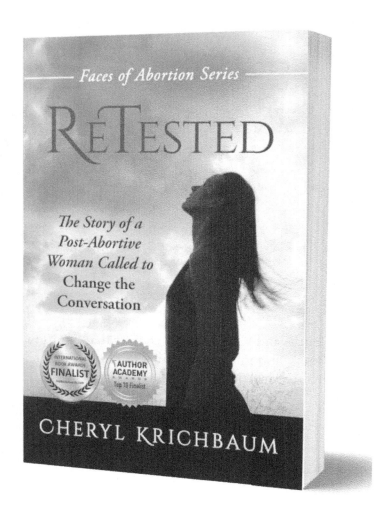

Faces of Abortion Series

ReTested

The Story of a
Post-Abortive
Woman Called to
Change the
Conversation

INTERNATIONAL BOOK AWARDS FINALIST

AUTHOR ACADEMY AWARDS Top 10 Finalist

CHERYL KRICHBAUM

Award-winning
ReTested
CHERYL KRICHBAUM
ReTestedBook.com

The **Missing** *Sex Ed Lessons*

Faith- and science-based courses that equip tweens, teens, and unmarried adults to delay sexual encounters so that they avoid:

- ☑ STIs/STDs
- ☑ Crisis pregnancies
- ☑ Challenging relationships

*O*nline *C*ourses
completed in the privacy
of your own home

MybodyMyworship.com

Made in the USA
Coppell, TX
19 March 2021

51962746R00115